INPUT / OUTPUT

INPUT / OUTPUT

*Some
Thoughts
for
Today
by
Orley R. Herron
and
Betty Alexander*

MOODY PRESS

CHICAGO

For Dad and Mom Herron
Wisdom, Inspiration—Love

For the members of the Now generation—
particularly my own Jeff and Sue, Dana, and
Nancy Alexander

PREFACE

During my last year as dean of students at Westmont College, Santa Barbara, California, I felt a great need to write a devotional book designed for modern man and the youth of today. The development of the manuscript took considerable time and I invited Betty Alexander, gifted Bible teacher, writer, and wife of William C. Alexander, a renowned Christian businessman, to assist me in the document. Her able and adept skills were so helpful in the formation of the manuscript that I asked her to be co-author, a position she rightfully deserved.

It is our desire that this manuscript will have a pronounced effect on those who read it by helping them to understand more clearly the power of the incomparable Christ and the unparalleled strength of the Word of God. The dedication of the book is shared by both authors and is so recognized on the dedicatory page.

ORLEY R. HERRON

"Thy word have I hid in my heart, that I might not sin against thee" (Ps. 119:11).

The Christian life is exactly like the life of the world in this one regard: We will get out of it exactly what we put into it. As we hide the Word of God in our hearts (Input) we will not only be kept from sin, we will also begin to show forth the fruits of the Spirit (Output) which are love, joy, peace, longsuffering, gentleness, goodness, faith, meekness, and self-control (Gal. 5:22).

"Yea, hath God said . . . ?" (Gen. 3:1).

The authenticity of the Scripture is the basis of Christianity. Without it we would know almost nothing about the Christ who *is* Christianity. The devil knows if he can take away our faith in the authority of the Word, our faith in Christ will soon follow. He started this project in the Garden of Eden and has been working on it ever since. When you hear those voices today saying, "Yea, hath God said?" remember where they come from.

❧　❧　❧

"Yea, hath God said . . . ?" (Gen. 3:1).

This apparently innocent question is loaded with devilish subtlety. A question always implies doubt. What Satan is most anxious to do is to bring us to doubt whether God has spoken. If He has not spoken or revealed Himself, how can we know Him or His will? This same question is being asked today by those who scoff at the idea of ultimate inspiration and authority. The terminology may be different, but remember the source is the same.

"Yea, hath God said, Ye shall not eat of every tree of the garden?" (Gen. 3:1).

One of Satan's most successful maneuvers is to cast doubt upon the goodness of God. It is amazing how many Christians fall into this trap. Is your idea of God that He is a policeman who is restricting your every move and ready to punish your slightest infraction? Or do you envision Him as a spoilsport who doesn't want you to have any fun? If so, you have believed an insinuation by the devil. Christ said, "I am come that you may have life and that more abundantly" (John 10:10, free trans.).

❦ ❦ ❦

"She took of the fruit thereof, and did eat, and gave also unto her husband with her; and he did eat" (Gen. 3:6*b*).

Adam's sin was not in eating the fruit but in deciding against God. Someone has truly said, "We are not made to act, but to decide." It is for *whom* we decide that conditions how we act. We can choose either the Spirit of God (yielding to God's will), or the spirit of Satan (independence from God's will); there is no neutral ground in between. The consequence of a seemingly simple choice can be very far-reaching. If we really believed this, how different our decisions would be!

"And the Lord God called unto Adam, and said unto him, Where art thou?" (Gen. 3:9).

God was not asking this question as an angry judge, but as a grieving Father. Fellowship had been broken because of sin, and God was drawing Adam back to Himself in confession. What a picture of God's heart this is! He is ever seeking us, drawing us back into fellowship with Himself, even when we are hiding from Him. The same question comes to each one of us today in relationship to God. If you have wandered or drifted away, you can be sure that God is calling you back. Where art *thou?*

❦ ❦ ❦

"But unto Cain and to his offering he had not respect" (Gen. 4:5).

Cain believed in God; he even came to worship Him. But he wanted to do it on his terms. He brought the fruit of his hands (symbolic of works) instead of the slain animal which God required. The theology of Cain has many followers today. They want to come to God with the fruit of their hands and to reject the sacrifice of God's Son. But God has established the terms upon which He will be approached. The Bible says He not only had respect unto Cain's offering, but unto Cain.

"And he said, I know not: Am I my brother's keeper?" (Gen. 4:9*b*).

Too often in our relationship to others we have an attitude of "I don't care." What starts out as a protective mechanism, ends in a hardening of the heart, which is sin. This attitude is not of God. Contrast it with that of Christ as He wept over Jerusalem, the city which rejected Him. We must not protect ourselves from the hostile world around us, but instead show our Lord's love to it. To the question, "Am I my brother's keeper?" Christians must always answer, "Yes."

❦ ❦ ❦

"What hast thou done? The voice of thy brother's blood crieth unto me from the ground" (Gen. 4:10).

God was trying to make Cain face up to the seriousness of his sin. He was saying, "I know what you've done, do *you* know what you've done?" In spite of the extent of Cain's evildoing, God sought to restore him to Himself. Today God is still asking His erring children the same question: What have you done? Is there something in your life that God is asking you about and you need to put right? Remember, nothing is too bad to be forgiven by our loving Father.

"And Cain went out from the presence of the LORD . . . *and he builded a city"* (Gen. 4:16-17).

It is striking to notice that the first civilization was founded out of the presence of God. There was agriculture (v. 20), music (v. 21), there were artisans; in other words, culture, cleverness and progress. But God was not in their life. With independence from God came the inevitable result—rebellion against God. We are not so modern and different today, are we? Whenever man is glorified and made everything, it isn't long before God is minimized and made nothing. Culture and intellect are really God's gifts to human life which can and should be used to glorify Him.

❧　❧　❧

"Enoch walked with God" (Gen. 5:22a).

The Christian life is often called a walk. A walk implies steady progress and continuing fellowship. Enoch did not take a turn or two with God, then leave His company. He walked with God three hundred years! Hebrews 11:5 tells us about Enoch, that he had this testimony—that "he pleased God." May we also please God by the consistency of our walk with Him.

14

"Enoch walked with God" (Gen. 5:22).

What does it mean to walk with God? For one thing, it means agreement. Amos 3:3 asks, "Can two walk together, except they be agreed?" When we are talking about God and man, there must be a yielded will on man's part to the will of God. God did not conform to Enoch, but Enoch conformed to God. Walking with God means we stop walking our own way, that we abandon the world's way and follow the Lord's way.

❧ ❧ ❧

"And it repented the Lord *that he had made man on the earth, and it grieved him at his heart"* (Gen. 6:6).

"Grief" is a love word. You cannot grieve someone unless they love you. God is not reigning aloof in the universe, unconcerned with what concerns us. He loves us and, because He loves us, He is grieved at our sin. His love and grief were so great that He sent His Son to die for that sin in our behalf. Even after we have accepted this gift of God, the Bible warns us: "Grieve not the Holy Spirit" (Eph. 4:30, ASV). May we walk carefully in responsive love to God that we may not grieve Him by our sin.

"But Noah found grace in the eyes of the Lord*"* (Gen. 6:8).

What a splendid figure of solitary goodness Noah was! He was the one saint of his day. He shows us that it is possible to be good even if we stand alone. It is possible to be right with God even in the midst of surrounding iniquity. How we need this word in the days in which we live! God is the same today as He was to Noah if only we are willing to fulfill the conditions.

❧   ❧   ❧

"Noah walked with God" (Gen. 6:9).

The Christian life is called a walk, not a hop, skip and jump. Some of us are great on the short dash but not much good on the long haul. We sing, "I'm following Jesus one step at a time," and that's what a walk is— one step at a time. There will be days when we can't see beyond the next step (and we're not meant to), but we will always be able to at least put one foot in front of the other. He always gives light for the next step.

"Noah walked with God" (Gen. 6:9).

Verse 5 tells us that "GOD saw that the wickedness of man was great in the earth, and that every imagination of the thoughts of his heart was only evil continually." It was in this kind of a world that we are told, "Noah walked with God." This took courage and independence as well as faith, for no one was walking that way. And when a man walks with God, he cannot walk with those who are going in the opposite direction. So, if you are in a hard place and the walk with God seems difficult in your circumstances, remember godly Noah who walked with God in a much harder place.

❧ ❧ ❧

"Thus did Noah; according to all that God commanded him, so did he" (Gen. 6:22).

What a statement to be made about anyone—that they were always obedient to the express will of God! And what Noah had been called upon to do was not an easy task. His faith in God cost Him a great deal. It was expensive in every way—in money, in time, in effort and in reputation. Let us ask ourselves, What is it costing me to express my faith in God? A faith that isn't costing anything isn't worth anything.

"And the Lord *said unto Noah, Come thou and all thy house into the ark"* (Gen. 7:1a).

This is the first time the word "come" is used in the Bible, but it occurs five hundred times. God always says, "Come," and "Come again." He never gets tired of receiving us; He never loses patience with us. God said, "Come" to Noah, not "Go," for He would be with him in the ark.

❧ ❧ ❧

"And Ham, the father of Canaan, saw the nakedness of his father, and told his two brethren without. And Shem and Japheth took a garment, and laid it upon both their shoulders, and went backward, and covered the nakedness of their father; and their faces were backward, and they saw not their father's nakedness" (Gen. 9:22-23).

Here we see a contrast in attitude toward sin in the family. One son "gazed in satisfaction" and "delighted in telling" (indicated in the original Hebrew) his father's sin, while the other brothers refused to even look upon it. How prone we are to take a secret pleasure in the failures of others and talk about it as well! This ought not to be, particularly in the family of God, for the Scripture says, "Love covereth a multitude of sins" (I Peter 4:8, ASV). Are we truly loving in this regard?

18

"Now the Lord had said unto Abram, Get thee out of thy country, and from thy kindred, and from thy father's house, unto a land that I will shew thee" (Gen. 12:1).

God's commands are seldom accompanied by reasons, but always by promises. Abram had to step out in faith and trust in God's faithfulness, believing that in God's good time His ultimate goal would be made known. Hebrews 11:8 tells us that "by faith Abraham, when he was called to go out into a place which he should after receive for an inheritance, obeyed; and he went out, not knowing whither he went." He did not know what the future held, but he knew who held the future. Can we say the same?

"Now the Lord had said unto Abram, Get thee out of thy country, and from thy kindred, and from thy father's house, unto a land that I will shew thee" (Gen. 12:1).

Sometimes we forget that when God's call came to Abram, he was not a godly man but an idolator. It was "not by works of righteousness" that he had done, but by His mercy God saved him. God did not ask Abram to clean up to be worthy of the call; the call came to him right where and as he was. However, obedience to the call required something on Abram's part; it required separation from his "world" and his natural place in it. So it will be for us—separation from the old way is the starting point of the life of faith.

"And there was a famine in the land" (Gen. 12:10*a*).

What a test of Abram's faith—famine in the land of promise! He must have wondered why God called him from the rich plains of Mesopotamia to this barren place. We are sometimes misled into identifying the peace and calm of outward circumstances with the peace which comes from being right with God. Difficulties do not necessarily mean we are out of God's will. The right way is not always the easiest way, and the easiest way is not always right. In any difficult situation, we should first ask ourselves, What does God want me to learn from this?

❧   ❧   ❧

"And there was a famine in the land: and Abram went down into Egypt to sojourn there" (Gen. 12:10).

This was a perfectly natural thing to do—to escape from a difficult situation. But Abram's position was not merely natural; he had a supernatural relationship with God. He was looking at the circumstances and forgetting the promises. He, who had journeyed all the way from Chaldea to Canaan because he believed God's word, was afraid to trust Him in time of famine. How like Abram we are! We believe God for the fate of our eternal soul but are afraid to trust Him for our daily problems.

"And he went on his journeys from the south even to Bethel, unto the place where his tent had been at the beginning, between Bethel and Hai; unto the place of the altar, which he had made there at the first: and there Abram called on the name of the LORD*"* (Gen. 13:3-4; read all of chap. 13).

In the time of famine, Abram had left Bethel, the place of worship and communion with God, to go down into Egypt, the place of worldliness and sin. He had acted in the wisdom of the flesh, which always suggests "a way out" instead of trusting God "within" the difficult circumstances. But He did not stay in Egypt. He returned to Bethel, to the altar of sacrifice and the fellowship with God. We can learn a great lesson from this patriarch of old. If you have left your Bethel and are wandering foolishly in Egypt, go back to the altar of sacrifice—the cross of Christ where you were "at first"—and call on the name of the Lord. He will receive you.

"And Lot lifted up his eyes, and beheld all the plain of Jordan, that it was well watered every where, before the Lord destroyed Sodom and Gomorrah, even as the garden of the Lord" (Gen. 13:10a).

Lot's whole life was conditioned by the choice he made at this point. What looked like the garden of the Lord to him was to the holy eye of God so wicked, it had to be destroyed. Lot did not seek the mind of God, nor did he see through His eyes. He made his decision on a purely carnal and natural level. This ended in disaster for himself and his family. We need to ask ourselves about our choices. By what are they motivated? Are they in line with the mind of God or are they just our natural desires?

"Lot . . . pitched his tent toward Sodom. But the men of Sodom were wicked and sinners before the Lord exceedingly" (Gen. 13:12b-13).

At first Lot only pitched his tent "toward Sodom," but soon we read, "Lot . . . dwelt in Sodom" (Gen. 14:12) and Lot "sat in the gate of Sodom" (19:1). We all know the horrible end of this story. How often do we pitch our tents toward some evil situation or companionship, feeling safe and confident that we can always extricate ourselves before we get too involved? All too soon we find ourselves "dwelling in Sodom" and "sitting at the gate"—totally immersed and identified with the situation. May we heed this warning example of Lot before we take that first step. We cannot play with sin without eventually becoming identified with it.

"And he believed in the Lord; and he counted it to him for righteousness" (Gen. 15:6).

This is the first appearance in the Bible of the word "believe" and it tells us a basic and essential truth. In the original Hebrew, "believe" comes from a root from which we get the English word "amen." In other words, Abram said "amen" to God. "Amen" is never a petition (May it be so) but always a word of strong agreement (So be it! It is so!). When Abram agreed with God, it was counted to him for righteousness. Abram had no original righteousness, but by his faith in God's word, he was "made right" with God. So it is with us when we say "Amen" to God.

❧ ❧ ❧

"Is any thing too hard for the Lord?" (Gen. 18:14).

In our prayer life we are so apt to look at the circumstances instead of at God. We are defeated by the "probabilities." If it doesn't seem "probable," we find it difficult to believe it can happen. But God is not only the God of the improbable, but of the impossible. We say, "If this or that could happen, it would be a miracle," forgetting that that is just the business God is in—the business of working miracles.

"Look not behind thee" (Gen. 19:17).

What a lesson we have in the story of Lot's wife! God offered her deliverance and a new life, but she preferred the things of this world and their accompanying sin. She died looking back and yearning after them. When God offers us deliverance from the sins of the world and the flesh, may we not look behind, but go on with Him.

❧ ❧ ❧

"And he said unto him, What is thy name? And he said, Jacob" (Gen. 32:27).

The name Jacob means "cheat." What God was really asking was, "Have you ever faced up to the kind of person you are?" Jacob answered honestly, "My life has been like my name." God is asking you, "What is your character, if you were to put it in one word?" Be honest—don't pretend to be something you're not. Say with Jacob, "Yes, I am like that, but I want to be like Christ." Then God can say, "Thy name shall be called no more Jacob, but Israel . . . a prince . . . with God" (Gen. 32:28).

"And Moses said, I will now turn aside, and see this great sight, why the bush is not burnt. And when the Lord saw that he turned aside to see, God called unto him out of the midst of the bush" (Exodus 3:3-4).

If you have never heard the call of God, perhaps it is because you have never "turned aside" long enough to hear His voice. It was after Moses made the conscious decision to "turn aside" that God called. James 4:8 says, "Draw nigh to God, and he will draw nigh to you." This is ever God's order. *You* "draw nigh" (an act of the will), and then see what God will do!

※　※　※

"And they gathered it every morning" (Exodus 16:21a).

We need to be stewards of our time as well as our money. As conditioned as we are to "cramming," we sometimes carry this habit over into our Christian life, with the same results that the Israelites had with the manna. Moses tells us that when they tried to hoard the manna, it "bred worms and stank." So it is with our spiritual food and blessing when we try to have "cramming sessions" with the Lord. We cannot hoard up grace, wisdom and peace for next week, or even tomorrow; neither can we live on yesterday's blessing. The manna must be gathered every morning. Daily we must meet the Lord.

"And God came unto Balaam, and said, What men are these with thee?" (Num. 22:9).

The men with Balaam could be called "doubtful companions." They were helpful financially, but detrimental spiritually. What kind of companions do you choose? Do they hinder your spiritual life? If so, better make a change.

꙳   ꙳   ꙳

"Choose you this day whom ye will serve" (Joshua 24:15).

The Christian life is a matter of choice. In every circumstance in which we find ourselves, we are confronted with this basic choice—to please ourselves, or to please God. These things are not always synonymous, but when we obey God we find we are also satisfied. Someone has truly said, "When I do as I please, I find I am not pleased with what I do."

"But Saul and the people spared Agag, and the best of the sheep, and of the oxen, and of the fatlings, and the lambs, and all that was good" (I Sam. 15:9).

God had said, "Utterly destroy all." But Saul said, "We will save the best," and in this fatal action lay the seeds of his own defeat. How like Saul we are! God says of the flesh, "Slay it all," but we want to kill the worst and spare the best. We want to get rid of the sins which impair our image, but cover the more subtle ones. If we do not obey God and "destroy it all," it will be the means of our continued defeat until we finally put it to death.

❧ ❧ ❧

"Wherefore then didst thou not obey the voice of the Lord, but didst fly upon the spoil, and didst evil in the sight of the Lord?" (I Sam. 15:19).

Saul was sent by God to fulfill a mission, but he failed because of partial obedience. This he tried to cover up with pious platitude and religious pretension. God was not deceived. To Him, partial disobedience is the same as disobedience, and Saul was rejected as king. We must take care that we do not throw up spiritual smoke screens to God as a substitute for true and complete obedience to His voice. God says, "To obey is better than sacrifice."

"And Samuel said, Hath the Lord as great delight in burnt-offerings and sacrifices, as in obeying the voice of the Lord? Behold, to obey is better than sacrifice, and to hearken than the fat of rams. For rebellion is as the sin of witchcraft, and stubbornness is as iniquity and idolatry" (I Sam. 15:22-23a).

We must be obedient to the light we have before God will give us any more light. Many Christians have frozen themselves at some low level of Christian experience because they have refused to obey God in some area of their lives. And so they live defeated, poverty-stricken lives, useless to God, and miserable to themselves and others. Like Cain, they are willing to offer sacrifices, but they are unwilling to obey. May our prayer be, "Lord, may we be willing to be made willing, that our lives be not an abomination to God."

"And Saul said unto Samuel, I have sinned: for I have transgressed the commandment of the Lord, and thy words: because I feared the people, and obeyed their voice" (I Sam. 15:24).

Who are you listening to? God, or the "people"? You cannot follow the voice of the crowd when they transgress the commandments of the Lord. If you do, the result will be the same as Saul's—rejection of God's highest calling from your life (v. 26). Even Paul recognized the possibility of becoming a spiritual castaway (I Cor. 9:27), a tragic condition for any Christian.

❧ ❧ ❧

"And Samuel came no more to see Saul until the day of his death: nevertheless Samuel mourned for Saul: and the Lord repented that he had made Saul king over Israel" (I Sam. 15:35).

There are no "has beens" in God's sight, only "might have beens." What is your condition right now? Are you willing to give of yourself completely to the Lord's leading, or are you holding back, hoping for other things to develop? God's leading demands an immediate response, so don't hesitate to yield. Failure to respond may place you in the "might have been" Christian celebrity row—an honor no Christian should desire.

"But the Lord said unto Samuel, Look not on his countenance, or on the height of his stature; because I have refused him: for the Lord seeth not as man seeth; for man looketh on the outward appearance, but the Lord looketh on the heart" (I Sam. 16:7).

We may be attracted to people whom God has refused for us. We may also reject—for superficial reasons—those of real spiritual depth who could be strengthening to us. All too often we make snap judgments about people. If they conform to our mold in speech and appearance, we accept them; if not, they are "chalked off." God's measuring stick of judgment is vastly different from ours. We should learn to judge others by *His* standards. Relationships more meaningful than we could imagine may result.

❧   ❧   ❧

"For the battle is the Lord's" (1 Sam. 17:47).

God wants us to be participants, not spectators, in the arena of life. We can be as fearless as David against just such unsurmountable odds because God has not changed. The God that delivered David, can and will deliver us from our enemies. David knew where his strength lay—not in sword or spear or shield, or any of man's defenses, but in the living God. He conquered because he knew "whom he had believed." This same victory is available to us.

"And it came to pass, when he had made an end of speaking unto Saul, that the soul of Jonathan was knit with the soul of David, and Jonathan loved him as his own soul" (I Sam. 18:1).

David and Jonathan had one of the finest relationships in all of the Old Testament Scripture. It is great to have a "Jonathan" in your life—one who is closer than a brother, one who accepts you as you are and would literally die for you. God, however, took Jonathan away from David. Be thankful for the "Jonathan" in your life, but never let him take the place of the Lord in directing and guiding your life.

❧   ❧   ❧

"And every one that was in distress, and every one that was in debt, and every one that was discontented, gathered themselves unto him; and he became a captain over them: and there were with him about four hundred men" (I Sam. 22:2).

Our tendency when we begin to doubt is to go for help to individuals who will reinforce our doubts. We must realize that where people will disappoint us, the Lord never will. Unfortunately we see people representing Christ, and we reject them as well as our caricature of Christ. We need to turn to Christ, not people, because His loving, consistent understanding is exactly what we need to help us face our doubts and problems, and to get rid of them.

"And he came thither unto a cave, and lodged there; and, behold, the word of the Lord came to him, and he said unto him, What doest thou here, Elijah?" (I Kings 19:9).

Elijah was hiding and running away from his spiritual responsibilities. God wanted him to face up to the fact that he *was* running away. He asks the same question of us today: What are you doing here? We can and must answer Him honestly, for God willingly meets us just where we are—not where we ought to be.

❧ ❧ ❧

"And I, even I only, am left; and they seek my life, to take it away" (I Kings 19:10*b*).

Are you depressed because you feel you are fighting the Christian battle alone? It is hard to be rejected or ostracized by the group. It will help you realize that this is not a new or unique experience among God's children, and many are sharing it with you right now. Remember how Elijah said, "Only I am left"? But God said: "Yet I have left me seven thousand in Israel, all the knees which have not bowed unto Baal, and every mouth which hath not kissed him" (I Kings 19:18). You also are not alone. Others have the same situation and are faithful in the midst of it.

"And he said, Go forth, and stand upon the mount before the Lord. And, behold, the Lord passed by, and a great and strong wind rent the mountains, and brake in pieces the rocks before the Lord; but the Lord was not in the wind: and after the wind an earthquake; but the Lord was not in the earthquake: and after the earthquake a fire; but the Lord was not in the fire: and after the fire a still small voice" (I Kings 19:11-12).

We are always looking for the earthquakes and the fire. We expect God to speak to us in some spectacular way, or we do not think He is speaking at all. Don't forget the still small voice. We must stay carefully and constantly "tuned in" to God to hear it. Let's not miss God's best for us because we are distracted by the noise around us and are following "other voices."

       🍀   🍀   🍀

"Fret not thyself" (Ps. 37:1a).

How many times we find ourselves at a place where many possibilities present themselves but we are unable to do anything about them! Our usual procedure is to allow our mind to go round and round like a squirrel in a cage, to uselessly fret and fume until we are exhausted and frustrated. We need to give the situation completely to the Lord and *leave* it with Him. Each time we are tempted to take it back, we must give it to Him again, until we are able to fret no more. He will show us His answer in His way and in His time, and it will always be the best answer for us.

"Delight thyself also in the Lord; and he shall give thee the desires of thine heart" (Ps. 37:4).

Man's best advice always falls short of God's omniscience. God can lead individuals to advise you and guide you; but remember, God has given you the opportunity to appropriate His guidance simply by the asking. God's standard of advice has eternal reliability and validity and has stood the test of time and experience. When one begins to yield to man's ways and desires, then God's wisdom is set aside. Saul began to yield to man's advice, and his relationship to God waned. So it will be with you.

❧ ❧ ❧

"Commit thy way unto the Lord; trust also in him; and he shall bring it to pass" (Ps. 37:5).

We can get trapped into making unwise decisions because of an unrealistic push to come to a conclusion by some deadline. God's timetable and man's timetable may be entirely different, and may not necessarily coincide. Moses waited eighty years before God permitted him to lead the people. Our task is not to run ahead of God. We simply commit our lives to Him and by faith trust the One who has brought those lives into being. At the proper time He will show us the next step we must take.

*"Commit thy way unto the Lord; trust also in him;
and he shall bring it to pass"* (Ps. 37:5).

Open doors do not necessarily mean that God wants
you to walk through them. It may be just a time to
reevaluate, and then to rededicate yourself to the task
at hand. Lay these choices before the Lord and have
"no opinion" of your own, so that He may not be ham-
pered in directing your final decision. Then, when
God clearly leads you to accept one path, you can
follow it with reckless, confident abandonment to the
promises of God.

❧   ❧   ❧

*"Why art thou cast down, O my soul? And why art
thou disquieted in me? Hope thou in God: for I shall
yet praise him for the help of his countenance"* (Ps.
42:5).

Depression is one of Satan's favorite weapons, and not
even the most mature or "spiritual" child of God is ex-
empt. While God's people cannot escape the "disease,"
they do have the remedy. Isaiah 61:3 tells us that God
"has given [past tense] the garment of praise for the
spirit of heaviness." Start praising and watch depression fall away!

"Be still, and know that I am God" (Ps. 46:10).

Most of us cannot be still before God because we have developed poor spiritual listening habits. Remember, it is impossible to listen and speak at the same time. Someone has said, "The Lord gave us two ears and one mouth because He wanted us to listen twice as much as we speak." We need to come into the Lord's presence without haste, preparing and quieting our hearts for our communion with Him. We must "be still" before we can truly know that He is God.

❧ ❧ ❧

"Cast thy burden upon the Lord, and he shall sustain thee: he shall never suffer the righteous to be moved" (Ps. 55:22).

When we come to the end of our own resources we have this wonderful promise from God! We do not need to stagger under the weight of our problems, but merely need to transfer the "load" onto Him. He has not promised to eliminate our problems but has promised to bear our burdens. He also has promised to hold us up and keep us steady. Can we ask for more?

"If riches increase, set not your heart upon them" (Ps. 62:10).

The Bible says, "The love of money is the root of all evil" (I Tim. 6:10). The issue is not whether a Christian should *have* money (it is not necessarily holy to be poor), but that he should not *love* money. Anything that takes the preeminence from God in our lives is wrong and is an idol. Riches may increase; and if they do, thank God for them. But these must not be the center of our love.

❧ ❧ ❧

"O sing unto the Lord a new song; for he hath done marvellous things: his right hand, and his holy arm, hath gotten him the victory" (Ps. 98:1).

God is a God of the positive. Some Christians create God as a God of the negative. True, God hates sin and any implication of it. However, He has chosen to deal with sin with an overwhelming, positive love in order to bring us to a realization of our helplessness and submit our lives to Him. This union with Christ centers not on the negative but on the positive things in life. This positive attitude results from God's joy, peace and contentment which are available for every believer. Satan is the ruler and creator of the negative and deceitful aspects of life. Make that distinction plain in your walk.

"O Lord, thou hast searched me, and known me. Thou knowest my downsitting and mine uprising, thou understandest my thought afar off. Thou compassest my path and my lying down, and art acquainted with all my ways. For there is not a word in my tongue, but, lo, O Lord, thou knowest it altogether" (Ps. 139:1-4).

God views each of us as an individual, totally responsible for our actions. He knows every sparrow that falls, every lily of the field that grows; and He is mindful of our every thought, whether it be hidden or public. Therefore, nothing is unknown to the Lord. Stop trying to hide—you can't. Open up the closet and clear out the garbage, and air it out before the Lord. He has promised to cleanse.

❧ ❧ ❧

"Trust in the Lord with all thine heart; and lean not unto thine own understanding" (Prov. 3:5-6).

How easy it is to become confused and perplexed today if we view the world around us without God's perspective. The Lord has promised that if we look to Him in complete trust, acknowledge Him in all that we do, and lean not on our own intelligence, He will direct each step we take. If you are at a stalemate, let the Lord have control. The confusion and perplexity will fall aside immediately.

"Wisdom is the principal thing: therefore get wisdom: and with all thy getting get understanding" (Prov. 4:7).

Knowledge of how to live the Christian life is not enough; the important thing is what quality of Christian life that knowledge produces. Knowing and doing are two different phases. Many possess knowledge of the Christian walk, but few travel the narrow road of discipleship. All the knowledge in all the world will not bring you any closer to the kingdom of God. It is the trusting, unabandoned giving of yourself daily to the Lord that He calls "understanding."

❧ ❧ ❧

"These six things doth the Lord hate: yea, seven are an abomination unto him: a proud look . . ." (Prov. 6:16-17a).

If we were to ask what sin we think God hates the most, we would perhaps come up with many diverse answers. But God puts pride at the top of the list. We may discover why when we realize that this sin is at the root and is the cause of all other sins. Pride takes so many forms and is so deceptive, it is possible for it to go undetected, particularly in ourselves. Let us examine our hearts before God and get rid of the pride He hates.

"For as he thinketh in his heart, so is he" (Prov. 23:7).

Our mind is an important part of our Christian experience, and the Bible has a great deal to say about it. Many think of Christianity as a matter of emotion. The truth is, it is largely a matter of the mind and will. If what we think determines what we are, then we must develop a habit of thinking thoughts and forming concepts that will purify and strengthen us, rather than those which will corrupt us or tear us down. The Scripture tells us in II Corinthians 10:5 to bring "into captivity every thought to the obedience of Christ." This takes an act of the will. The result is victory for God rather than Satan.

❧ ❧ ❧

"And he said, Go, and tell this people" (Isa. 6:9; read vv. 1-9).

How often are we challenged to witness with no mention of heart preparation? Before God gave Isaiah a commission to "go and tell," several things had already taken place. First, Isaiah had had a vision of God's holiness and his own uncleanliness (we never really see ourselves as sinners until we are set in the light of God's perfect purity). Second, confession and cleansing came, and then, God's call to go.

"In quietness and in confidence shall be your strength" (Isa. 30:15).

There is a temptation to "get" so busy "for the Lord" that we never have time to wait before Him and to hear what He has to say. Then we are surprised at how easily we fall into the snares of the devil. Confidence comes from knowing someone well enough to trust him. To know someone, you must listen to his voice; and to listen, you must be quiet.

❧ ❧ ❧

"And therefore will the Lord wait, that he may be gracious unto you" (Isa. 30:18).

God is trusting you to trust Him, and to learn to wait upon Him. His answers are "exceeding abundantly above all that we ask or think" (Eph. 3:20). God's silence may be testing your faith, and you can thank Him that He has entrusted us with His silence. These are the times when the deepest treasures of heaven and resources of God are at work in our lives. Don't run ahead of His answers and take things into your own hands. There are many promises for those who wait upon the Lord. Learn them and stand upon them!

"And therefore will the Lord wait, that he may be gracious unto you" (Isa. 30:18).

God has three answers to prayer—yes, no and not yet. Sometimes "not yet" seems to be the hardest answer of all. Scripture abounds in instructions to God's children to *wait*. God knows the perfectly right time. His infinite knowledge causes Him to deny some of our requests when we think they seem so logical and right. Many a Christian has walked a bitter and defeated road because he was not willing to wait and trust in the graciousness of God.

❧   ❧   ❧

"Behold, I will do a new thing" (Isa. 43:19).

Don't put God in a box. Let Him do a "new thing" with and for you. We are so afraid to depart from the accustomed way of living the Christian life that we can become listless and lifeless. God is a God of diversity. He purposely made you unlike any other person. God is creative; He wants you to be a creative Christian.

"Behold, the Lord's hand is not shortened, that it cannot save; neither his ear heavy, that it cannot hear: but your iniquities have separated between you and your God, and your sins have hid his face from you, that he will not hear" (Isa. 59:1-2).

Are you going through a period of "no answer to prayer"? Perhaps this verse explains the reason. The problem is never that God is unable to meet the need, nor is He unwilling. The problem is usually sin in the heart of the petitioner. Separation is always the result of sin, but God is waiting to answer prayer when we come to Him in true confession and penitence.

❧ ❧ ❧

"And it shall come to pass, that before they call, I will answer; and while they are yet speaking, I will hear" (Isa. 65:24).

Most of us have trouble with prayer. Sometimes we feel that our prayers are heard, and sometimes we feel as if they don't go above the ceiling. Remember that your "feelings" have nothing to do with the facts. God tells us that He *does* hear and that He *will* answer. Your feelings are unreliable, constantly changing. God's Word is eternal and never changing. Never trust feelings, only facts.

"For my people have committed two evils; they have forsaken me the fountain of living waters, and hewed them out cisterns, broken cisterns, that can hold no water" (Jer. 2:13).

We often hear the statement "It is better to have faith in something than nothing." What a ridiculous conclusion that is! We have all had the experience of having faith in the wrong persons or causes, and have found how heartbreaking and expensive it can be. Someone has truly said, "Faith is a bucket let down in a well. What good is a bucket if the well is empty?" Let us not put our faith in the empty wells and broken cisterns of the world, but trust to the fountain of living waters, which is Christ.

❧ ❧ ❧

"And the vessel that he made of clay was marred in the hand of the potter: so he made it again another vessel, as seemeth good to the potter to make it" (Jer. 18:4).

Paul tells us we are to be vessels "unto honour, sanctified, and meet for the master's use" (II Tim. 2:21). All too often, when the master Potter is forming us as His vessels, He comes across some hard place that makes us unusuable for His purpose. If He cannot work this hardness out of us, He will have to break us down and begin again. But He never rejects us, for the conforming work is His work. He *will* perform it! (Phil. 1:6).

"But the people that do know their God shall be strong, and do exploits" (Dan. 11:32*b*).

As you read this verse, you may be saying, "But you don't know how weak I am." What sometimes passes for humility is really lack of faith. The secret of strength is not in yourself, but in your knowledge of God. You, indeed, may be weak, but think who He is! Get to know Him through prayer and His Word; then you will "do exploits."

❧ ❧ ❧

"And he answered and spake unto those that stood before him, saying, Take away the filthy garments from him. And unto him he said, Behold, I have caused thine iniquity to pass from thee, and I will clothe thee with change of raiment" (Zech. 3:4).

The Bible tells us that our righteousnesses are as filthy rags in God's sight (Isa. 64:6). When we acknowledge this, He gives us a change of raiment, even the "garments of salvation" and "the robe of righteousness" (Isa. 61:10). What an exchange—our filthy rags for His spotless garments! What is the condition of your spiritual apparel?

"Then was Jesus led up of the spirit into the wilderness to be tempted of the devil" (Matt. 4:1).

Temptation is not sin, for Christ Himself was tempted and was without sin (Heb. 4:15). It was the Holy Spirit who led Jesus up into the wilderness to be tempted of the devil. God uses even these temptations for our good. The devil tempts us to destroy us, but God tests us to strengthen us.

🍀 🍀 🍀

"Blessed are they which do hunger and thirst after righteousness: for they shall be filled" (Matt. 5:6).

Miles Sanford said, "Failure where self is concerned in our Christian life is allowed and often engineered by God in order to turn us completely from ourselves unto His source for our lives: Christ Jesus who never fails." What an encouraging word that is! We can be sure that even our stumblings and fallings are blessing from our loving Father who wants us to be aware of our need of Him. Be glad, then, of your need and hunger of heart. You have a promise from God—you shall be filled!

"And whosoever shall compel thee to go a mile, go with him twain" (Matt. 5:41).

We must learn to go the second mile and learn to do it joyfully. Just doing our "Christian duty" isn't enough. When we truly follow Jesus, we give up all rights to ourselves—to our privacy, our time, our energy— just as He did. Though it is true that we must be good stewards of these things and not waste them, we will often have to spend them in the behalf of others. Remember, Jesus "did not cling to his prerogatives as God's equal," but gladly relinquished them for our salvation (Phil. 2:6, Phillips). So we must do if we are to be His disciples.

❧ ❧ ❧

"But I say unto you, Love your enemies, bless them that curse you, do good to them that hate you, and pray for them which despitefully use you, and persecute you" (Matt. 5:44).

Can you ever really love your enemies? The answer is *no—you* cannot. But Christ can, and does and will *through* you if you will allow Him to. Paul said, "The love of Christ constraineth us." It was not his love but Christ's love that flowed through him to others. Stop trying to do it yourself—your natural love can never encompass the unlovely and hateful. But God's love is perfect and unconditional, and it is yours for the taking.

". . . *that they may have glory of men*" (Matt. 6:2).

The world is full of fakes—people who pretend to be what they are not. Jesus calls these hypocrites. This characteristic is easy to spot in others, but not as easy to spot in ourselves. We are all dangerously close to becoming hypocrites. The world needs no new addition to that illustrious group. Ask yourself how many "spiritual" things you engage in because they bring the "glory of man." Jesus said, "Be not as the hypocrites."

❧   ❧   ❧

"*But seek ye first the kingdom of God, and his righteousness; and all these things shall be added unto you*" (Matt. 6:33).

When we earnestly seek the things of God, the other "things" come after. They are "added unto us" after we get in line with God's program. We may be tempted into expediency as a shortcut to gain spiritual goals, but spiritual ends are never gained by worldly means. First we must seek the kingdom of God, then God can bless us with "things" if this is in His plan.

"And why beholdest thou the mote that is in thy brother's eye, but considerest not the beam that is in thine own eye?" (Matt. 7:3).

One thing that Jesus most often condemned was the sin of judgment, yet Christians most readily fall into this. Hiding behind a front of so-called honesty, we are cruel and critical with one another. This ought not to be. Christ alone is to be our Judge. Before we analyze the deficiencies of others, let us examine our own lives. Oswald Chambers says, "God never gives us the gift of discernment that we may criticize, but that we may intercede."

❧ ❧ ❧

"And when he was entered into a ship, his disciples followed him. And, behold, there arose a great tempest in the sea" (Matt. 8:23-24a).

The disciples followed Jesus and were led into a great tempest! This reveals to us a spiritual principle: even storms are in the will of God. So often we have the misconception that if we are "following Jesus" there will be no problems. Not so. It is in these very times that we learn to experience the calming presence of Jesus. In this way, as in no other, we get to know who He is and what He can do.

"And he saith unto them, Why are ye fearful, O ye of little faith? Then he arose, and rebuked the winds and the sea; and there was a great calm" (Matt. 8:26).

Has the Lord led you to take the step of faith and enter into a new experience? Don't let the newness unsettle or discourage you; all of us resist change. But God will bring you into perfect rest if you place your trust in His ability to still the storm.

                  ❧   ❧   ❧

"They that be whole need not a physician, but they that are sick" (Matt. 9:12b).

The thing that recommends us to God is our need. If we do not know we are sick, we can never be made whole. We may all recognize this as we initially come with our sin to Christ for salvation, yet we do not realize that the principle continues throughout our Christian life. We can become smug and complacent and not be alert to our spiritual ills. But as we are made aware of our need by the Holy Spirit, how wonderful it is to know that the great Physician is ever ready to heal!

*"No man putteth a piece of new cloth unto an old gar-
ment, for that which is put in to fill it up taketh from
the garment, and the rent is made worse"* (Matt. 9:16).

The Bible does not teach reformation, but regenera-
tion through faith in Christ. God does not want to
make us over; He wants to make us new. He has
utterly rejected the "old man," telling us to put on the
"new man," which is Christ in us. "If any man be in
Christ, he is a new creature" (II Cor. 5:17), not a
"patched up" old one. Christianity is not a do-it-your-
self project; it's a job only God can do, so let Him do it.

❧ ❧ ❧

"He that is not with me is against me" (Matt. 12:30).

In our relationship to Christ we cannot be "on the
fence"; there is no such position in the Christian life.
We are either for Christ or against Him. We may not
deny our Lord as Peter did with an oath, but we can
deny Him just as surely by a closed mouth. Let us
speak when we need to speak, and be "for" what we
need to be "for."

"And he did not many mighty works there because of their unbelief" (Matt. 13:58).

What a sobering thought—we can actually limit almighty God through our unbelief! How many times we see a lack of power manifested in our Christian experience. As we look around us, no "mighty works" are being done. God does not seem to be working, and we wonder why. You can be sure the problem is not with God. Perhaps if we look into our own hearts we will find the answer. Are we believing His Word, standing on His promises, expecting Him to act in answer to prayer? Or are we filled with unbelief?

❧   ❧   ❧

"This is my beloved Son, in whom I am well pleased; hear ye him" (Matt. 17:5).

There has always been a multitude of voices crying for attention. Some have good things to say which are profitable for our hearing; some have dangerous things to say which confuse us and lead us away from God. We must be constantly evaluating the things we hear— choosing the good and eliminating the bad. How can we be sure of our choices? One infallible test is, How does it measure up with what Christ has said? In the final analysis, He is the One we must hear as a Guide for our lives.

"And Jesus went into the temple of God, and cast out all them that sold and bought in the temple, and overthrew the tables of the moneychangers, and the seats of them that sold doves. And said unto them, It is written, My house shall be called the house of prayer; but ye have made it a den of thieves" (Matt. 21:12-13).

Just as the temple was a special dwelling place of God in Old Testament times, the New Testament tells us that our bodies become the temple of God when Christ comes in. The temple is to be a place of blessing and prayer. What have you made of it? Is it used for your own purposes, or the purposes of God? Jesus never asks us to cleanse our own temples, but He does claim the right to come in and do the job for us. Let the "house cleaning" begin.

❧ ❧ ❧

"For this is my blood of the new testament, which is shed for many for the remission of sins" (Matt. 26:28).

Salvation by the shed blood of Christ is no more popular a teaching today than it was when it was taught by the lips of Jesus Himself. It has been denied, rejected or merely ignored by many persons from that day to this. How strange it is, for each time communion is taken it is a testimony to belief in the shed blood of Christ. How sad it is that there are actually those who are offended by the very sacrifice which was made on their behalf out of the great heart of God's love. Jesus said, "Doth this offend you?" (John 6:61).

"And he said unto her, Daughter, thy faith hath made thee whole" (Mark 5:34).

Was it her faith alone that made this woman whole? No, it was her faith *in* Him and His power to do what He said. Faith must have an object, and that object must be worthy of faith for results to take place. Nor is it the quantity of your faith that is important. Jesus said it could be as small as a grain of mustard seed. No, it is the object of your faith that counts. When we put our faith in Christ, we can be confident that He is worthy.

❧ ❧ ❧

"And he looked up, and said, I see men as trees, walking. After that he put his hands again upon his eyes, and made him look up: and he was restored, and saw every man clearly" (Mark 8:24-25).

This is a story of a blind man whose eyes were opened up by Jesus. At first he only saw "men as trees, walking," but at Christ's second touch, he saw "every man clearly." Are we guilty of seeing those about us in just as incomplete a way as this blind man saw them—as blurred outlines, lacking identity and reality? Are we as blind spiritually as this man was blind physically? Perhaps we too should have a "second touch" from God that we may see "every man clearly" as an individual with specific needs. Perhaps we need our eyes opened by Jesus so that we may see men as He sees them.

"And he said to them all, If any man will come after me, let him deny himself, and take up his cross daily, and follow me" (Luke 9:23).

We often hear Christians say in martyred tones, "Well, that is my cross to bear," referring to some difficulty or trial in their lives. This is not the cross of which Christ is speaking. The taking up of the cross is, in His words, "denying self"—the daily giving up of our life and dying to self that Paul speaks of when he says, "I die daily" (I Cor. 15:31).

※   ※   ※

"Nevertheless not my will, but thine, be done" (Luke 22:42).

Jesus is to be our Example in this way above all: His complete dependence upon the Father. He constantly reiterated, "I can do nothing of myself," "I do only what I see of the Father." His will was completely submitted to God, even unto that final excruciating test in the garden. Few of us have ever been put to that extremity in choosing the will of God. Why does it seem so hard for us to yield up our will to Him? Because we have so thoroughly enthroned self (which is flesh spelled backward without the "h") in the place of God.

"What seek ye?" (John 1:38).

On many occasions Christ asked the question, What seek ye? He asked this question of Andrew and Peter because He wanted those men to be perfectly clear about what they were after. Christ asks the same question of us: What seek ye? Our response must be given in the light of Calvary, and understood in the shadow of the cross. We will then say, I seek Christ and His will to be exemplified perfectly in my life.

❧ ❧ ❧

"One of the two which heard John speak, and followed him, was Andrew, Simon Peter's brother. He first findeth his own brother Simon, and saith unto him, We have found the Messias, which is, being interpreted, the Christ. And he brought him to Jesus" (John 1:40-42a).

Thank God for the Andrews. Every time Andrew is mentioned in Scripture, he is referred to as Simon Peter's brother; yet Christ used him in very significant ways. Andrew brought Simon Peter to Jesus. He also brought the lad to Christ whose little lunch was to feed the five thousand. Christ may have an "Andrew plan" for your life and, if so, thank Him for it. God has given you a very special purpose in this world. Remember, those that have been given the spotlight may not have the blessings and spiritual rewards of the Andrews.

58

"Thou art . . . thou shalt be" (John 1:42).

Andrew brought Simon to Jesus and that meeting transformed his life. Christ told him that day, "Thou art Simon, the son of Jona: thou shalt be called Cephas, which is by interpretation, A stone." He was changed from a faltering Simon, to rocklike Cephas. This same transformation is available to you. No matter how weak or unstable you may be, God's power is not limited by your inadequacies. If you will give your life to Him, He will change it from "thou art" to the "thou shalt be."

   ॐ   ॐ   ॐ

"For God so loved the world" (John 3:16).

Unfortunately, all too often we see Christians who possess sound doctrine but also are negative, censorious, proud and unappealing. No wonder the world says, "If that's Christianity, who needs it!" Is that Christianity? It certainly is not! These are the very attitudes Jesus Himself condemned in the religious Pharisees. Let us be careful that our possession of "right doctrine" does not produce in us an attitude of critical pride instead of loving concern to those who are "without." "God so loved the world"; we cannot do less.

"For Jesus himself testified, that a prophet hath no honour in his own country" (John 4:44).

Are you discouraged because those around you are not as enthusiastic about Christ as you are? Remember, Jesus Himself had no honor in His own country. Even His family rejected Him, and this may be your experience too. Your job is to be a good witness in life and word; conversion is the job of the Holy Spirit. You do the praying, and leave the results to Him. His purposes *will* be worked out.

❧ ❧ ❧

"Verily, verily, I say unto you, He that heareth my word, and believeth on him that sent me, hath everlasting life, and shall not come into condemnation; but is passed from death unto life" (John 5:24).

Some individuals say, "I have been 'born again.'" Others use the term "saved"; and some say, "I have had a 'spiritual encounter.'" The question to be answered is: Is the life of Christ being manifested in you? This is a present-tense situation. Eternal life is something we have *right now,* not just after we die. You either have life or you don't. The definition for eternal life is in John 17:3: "And this is life eternal, that they might know thee the only true God, and Jesus Christ, whom thou hast sent." Christianity is a matter of life and death.

"When Jesus therefore perceived that they would come and take him by force, to make him a king, he departed again into a mountain himself alone" (John 6:15).

There are times when we need to withdraw ourselves from a situation. All of us have a tendency to get into situations from which we cannot disentangle ourselves. Retreat is not always the mark of a coward. Too many times we stay to fight certain circumstances and come out bearing the scars of intense battle. Christ gave us a wonderful example when the people desired to make Him king and yet He withdrew from their midst. If God tells us to withdraw, we need not concern ourselves with what people think.

❧   ❧   ❧

"Many therefore of his disciples, when they had heard this, said, This is an hard saying; who can hear it?" (John 6:60).

Faith not only relies upon the precious promises of God, but believes His solemn warnings. We cannot pick and choose in God's Word, believing only what appeals to us. It is very popular today to say, "God is love." Yes, God is love, but He hates sin. He has condemned it and will judge it. We must believe this to be saved ourselves from this judgment and to be truly concerned for the fate of others.

61

"If any man will do his will, he shall know of the doctrine, whether it be of God, or whether I speak of myself" (John 7:17).

All of us need to have discernment between right and wrong, good and better, better and best. Often we settle for a good thing which is really the enemy of the best. Our natural intuition is not sufficient or reliable in discerning God's will. We need to submit our plans to Him and ask Him to guide us by His Spirit. Then we will know God's best for us.

❧   ❧   ❧

"Jesus stood and cried, saying, If any man thirst, let him come unto me, and drink" (John 7:37b).

Do you feel your limitations so keenly that you dare not believe you could ever be an overflowing Christian? Jesus has made this offer to "any man." There is only one prerequisite—the prerequisite of need; you must "thirst." Your very emptiness is what makes you eligible for all the fullness of God. When we have this intense desire—this thirst—we need only come to Him and be satisfied. After we have "taken in," we will be able to "give out" to others, for there is an abundant and ever renewing supply in Christ.

"He that believeth on me, as the scripture hath said, out of his belly shall flow rivers of living water" (John 7:38).

When we come to Christ to be filled, we are not to become sponges, just taking in, but we are to become rivers, flowing out to others. Unfortunately many of us are more like taps which only drip occasionally. Wherever a river flows, there is life. It is a transforming, life-giving influence. What kind of influence are we upon those around us?

❧ ❧ ❧

"I must work the works of him that sent me, while it is day: the night cometh, when no man can work" (John 9:4).

We have only one life to live on earth. Once that life is over, we are in eternity and can do no more. Don't wait to serve the Lord. God says, "Now is the accepted time." Don't put off yielding and responding to the voice of God, or the blessing will be lost. We do not get more tender to the things of the Spirit; but as the years go by, we harden. Don't let your life be a "what could have been," but a "what is" by God's grace and power.

"I am come that they might have life, and that they might have it more abundantly" (John 10:10*b*).

Satan is the accuser of God to man and man to God. His oldest weapon is to tell us that God wants to deprive us of something. He used this line with Eve in the garden and he hasn't changed it since, because it worked so well. Are we going to believe Satan as Eve did with the same sure results, or are we going to believe God, who tells us He wants to give us abundant life?

     ❧   ❧   ❧

"Abide in me, and I in you" (John 15:4*a*).

It takes clock hours to get to know someone. Only by spending time with them do we begin to understand them, love them and become like them. The Christian life is the same adventure to get to know, to love and to understand Christ's will for our lives. We must regularly meet Him. The more we love a person, the more we want to be with him. This is true of our growth in Christ. The more we learn of His majesty and our inheritance, the more we will seek His face. Without communication, friendships diminish. May it never be so in our relationship to Christ.

"Without me ye can do nothing" (John 15:5).

All of us have a longing to be independent, and God made us this way. God has given us this independent will, but it was this very thing that caused Adam and Eve to sin. God wants to move you out of independence (which is dependence upon "self") into dependence upon Him. Are you in a state of spiritual independence, trying to manipulate your own life in your own way? Remember that independence is the religion of hell.

❧ ❧ ❧

"If ye abide in me, and my words abide in you, ye shall ask what ye will, and it shall be done unto you" (John 15:7).

Some of us pray to God as if He were a celestial bellboy. We expect Him to run to answer our every selfish demand. All the promises for answered prayer have long strings attached. First ask, Do I meet the requirements? If we are abiding in Him and His words are abiding in us, *then* our requests will quite naturally be in conformity to His will, and our prayers will be answered.

"These things have I spoken unto you, that my joy might remain in you, and that your joy might be full" (John 15:11).

All of us are subject to depression at one time or another, but depression that continues always means we are "out of joint" with God. Christ has promised that in Him our joy may be full. When the joy leaves and the gloom takes over, we must ask ourselves why. The trouble is always on our side of the relationship—not on God's. We must go back in our experience until we find the place where we stepped out of the Lord's will, confess it, and get back to abiding in Him.

✄   ✄   ✄

"Howbeit when he, the Spirit of truth, is come, he will guide you into all truth" (John 16:13).

Truth is seeing things as they really are. The Spirit of truth, who indwells every Christian, unfolds to each one of us the nature of reality. Christians should then be the most realistic of all people. Worldings cannot understand reality, because the whole dimension of spiritual truth is closed to them.

"Howbeit when he, the Spirit of truth, is come, he will guide you into all truth" (John 16:13).

If you are a Christian, never say you cannot understand the Bible. The Bible is not a riddle but a revelation. God has given it to you that you may know Him and His will. He has also given you His Spirit in order that you may be able to understand it. He *will* guide into all truth. That's a promise; lay hold of it.

※　※　※

"And this is life eternal, that they might know thee the only true God, and Jesus Christ, whom thou hast sent" (John 17:3).

Being a Christian is not agreeing to a set of doctrines; rather, it is knowing a Person. It is possible to be doctrinally sound and spiritually dead. Mental assent to truth is not enough; we must know Him who is truth. Do you know Him in a personal way?

"And ye shall be witnesses unto me both in Jerusalem, and in all Judaea, and in Samaria, and unto the uttermost part of the earth" (Acts 1:8).

We are to be witnesses *first* to Jerusalem, which is right where we are. This is often the hardest place. But if we cannot be missionaries across the street, we will never be missionaries across the ocean. Look around you and be aware of the needs of your Jerusalem. Start giving out the message now. The fields are white unto harvest and the laborers are few.

❀ ❀ ❀

"We cannot but speak the things which we have seen and heard" (Acts 4:20).

Our witness for Christ should be the spontaneous result of our walk with Him. It should be the overflow of His life within us, not something we have dredged up from the bottom of the barrel because of duty. If Christ is the center of our interest, we will naturally want to share Him with others. Do you speak easily about your Saviour? If not, why not?

"For I am not ashamed of the gospel of Christ: for it is the power of God unto salvation to every one that believeth" (Rom. 1:16).

To some, the Christian life is a life of defeat and frustration because they are ashamed to let others know of their relationship to Christ. Christ's desire for every believer is that their witness will be a vital, magnetic and unashamed experience. The reason we are ashamed is that we really do not believe that the gospel "is the power of God unto salvation." If we will lay hold of this truth, we will be filled with excitement and anticipation in our every contact, for we will be waiting to see God's power exhibited. We are part of a wonderful plan God has for the redemption of the lost. He wants each of us to be a channel for His power. Believe it and act in it.

"For when we were yet without strength, in due time Christ died for the ungodly. But God commendeth his love toward us, in that, while we were yet sinners, Christ died for us" (Rom. 5:6, 8).

Christ knows you and accepts you just as you are. He knows your sin and your inability to rectify it. That is why He died for you! Come to Him with all your doubts and weaknesses and let Him transform your life. He has won the victory, and the victory can be yours because you have the Victor.

❧   ❧   ❧

"For I know that in me (that is, in my flesh,) dwelleth no good thing" (Rom. 7:18a).

The trouble with most of our Christian lives is that we have never accepted God's assessment of our "old man" as having nothing salvable. We all acknowledge that there are many things in our flesh we would gladly be rid of, but there are other things we feel we can improve, dress up, or that aren't "too bad" just the way they are. We would like to rewrite the verse to read "in my flesh dwelleth *some* good thing." But God has said "no good thing" and until we agree with Him in this condemnation of the flesh or self-life, there can be no liberation of the Christ-life in our Christian experience.

"For I know that in me (that is, in my flesh,) dwelleth no good thing: for to will is present with me; but how to perform that which is good I find not" (Rom. 7:18).

After we are ensnared by Satan, we promise the Lord that we will never get into the same difficulty again. Then we find ourselves caught in the same sin, and we go down to defeat again. Why? Because we still have confidence in the flesh. Anytime you put your confidence in the flesh, you will lose. Put your trust in the changeless person of Christ. The Scripture says that "I can do all things through Christ which strengtheneth me" (Phil. 4:13). The key is that *Christ* is the strength, not you.

      ჰ   ჰ   ჰ

"There is therefore now no condemnation to them which are in Christ Jesus, who walk not after the flesh, but after the Spirit" (Rom. 8:1).

What liberating words these are! And this includes self-condemnation. Many a Christian is under bondage to this sin. If we condemn ourselves, it shows we still expect something of ourselves, and have not accepted God's death sentence upon our "old man." When we accept our position as "dead indeed unto sin, but alive unto God" (Rom. 6:11), then we experience the liberty of "no condemnation."

"There is therefore now no condemnation to them which are in Christ Jesus, who walk not after the flesh, but after the Spirit" (Rom. 8:1).

This includes self-condemnation. Don't be more "spiritual" than God. He has forgiven you; now forgive yourself. We may need self-examination to recognize our sin, which will lead us to confession before God. We do not need self-condemnation, which always leads us to depression, defeat and alienation from God.

❧ ❧ ❧

"They that are in the flesh cannot please God" (Rom. 8:8).

The flesh will do anything to survive, even become religious! What it will not do is surrender or die of its own accord; it must be put to death. There will be no deliverance for us until we agree with God and pronounce the death sentence. When we are dead to the self-life, we are at last alive to the Christ-life within.

"The Spirit itself beareth witness with our spirit, that we are the children of God" (Rom. 8:16).

The spiritual vacuum in man raises the question, Is there a God? Christians respond with a heartfelt and confident "yes." If you have witness of the Spirit, do not let philosophical or theological arguments unsettle you. Remember, a man with an experience is never at the mercy of a man with an argument.

❧ ❧ ❧

"The Spirit itself beareth witness with our spirit, that we are the children of God: and if children, then heirs; heirs of God, and joint-heirs with Christ; if so be that we suffer with him, that we may be also glorified together" (Rom. 8:16-17).

You are God's rich relatives; stop living like His poor relatives. Think of what you possess—not just in that great day of glorification, but right now! Not only are we children of the King; we are joint-heirs with Christ. Truly "all things" are ours (I Cor. 3:21), but even "all things" are valueless to us unless we appropriate them by faith and make them real in our lives. Start possessing your possessions.

"Likewise the Spirit also helpeth our infirmities: for we know not what we should pray for as we ought: but the Spirit itself maketh intercession for us with groanings which cannot be uttered. And he that searcheth the hearts knoweth what is the mind of the Spirit, because he maketh intercession for the saints according to the will of God" (Rom. 8:26-27).

True prayer is not a natural human activity. It is not something we can think up ourselves or carry on ourselves. Because of this, God has given us the Holy Spirit to "help our infirmities." The way He does this is to take over completely and do our praying for us. Stop "trying to pray" and let the Holy Spirit do it for you. You will then be praying in accordance with the will of God, and He can and will answer you.

"And we know that all things work together for good to them that love God, to them who are the called according to his purpose" (Rom. 8:28).

This is an easy verse to quote glibly concerning the problems of others, but one not so easy to apply to the difficulties that confront us in our Christian life. How can this verse be true? We can only understand the truth of it in connection with verse 29: "For whom he did foreknow, he also did predestinate to be conformed to the image of his Son." Here is the "good" for which God is working all things together. We equate good with comfort, pleasure and success; God equates good with conforming us to the image of His Son. It is our *spiritual* good that God is interested in.

❧   ❧   ❧

"For whom he did foreknow, he also did predestinate to be conformed to the image of his Son" (Rom. 8:29).

We are changing every second of our lives although we may not be aware of it. This is also true in the spiritual realm. We never stand still. Examine your spiritual condition. Are you progressing or retrogressing from God's standpoint? What we regard as the process, He regards as the goal. His goal is to conform you to the image of His Son. How is the conforming process coming?

75

"For whom he did foreknow, he also did predestinate to be conformed to the image of his Son" (Rom. 8:29).

Too often we struggle to know God's will and forget that His will is for us to know Him and to be conformed to the image of His Son. Our efforts can be so easily dissipated in fruitless activity. If we know Him and are being conformed to His image, we will not need to concern ourselves about His will for our lives.

❧   ❧   ❧

"For whom he did foreknow, he also did predestinate to be conformed to the image of his Son" (Rom. 8:29).

Generally we identify with people who are most like ourselves, or whom we desire to be like. As a newborn babe in Christ, we must learn early to identify with Christ and desire to be like Him. He is our Example. Satan would have us identify with those who are most like our "old man" so that our carnal nature will be fed and our spiritual nature weakened. Be alert to the dangers of feeding the "old man" through poor associations.

"So then faith cometh by hearing, and hearing by the word of God" (Rom. 10:17).

Faith is a much abused word, even among Christians. Many seem to think that you either have it or you don't; and if you don't, there's really no help for it. Or some feel it's something they long for and hope for, and think that perhaps some day it may descend upon them. God has given us a simple formula for faith. You get it by hearing the Word of God. Do you want faith? Expose yourself to the Bible, and faith will come.

❧ ❧ ❧

"Don't let the world around you squeeze you into its own mold, but let God remold your minds from within, so that you may prove in practice that the plan of God for you is good, meets all his demands and moves toward the goal of true maturity" (Rom. 12:2, Phillips).

Groups have a great influence upon us. We dress alike, think alike and talk alike because the group will accept us if we do these things. Before long we lose our spiritual identity and we become indistinguishable. Too often the goals of the group are contrary to God's standards; and, as a result, we compromise our witness for Christ. Remember, a Christian is always running contrary to the mores of the world. We are in truth a minority group, but God and one believer make a majority.

"O Lord, thou hast searched me, and known me" (Ps. 139:1).

The word "personality" has its root in the word "mask." All human personality involves the wearing of three masks. These are: what we think we are, what others think we are, and what we really are. God sees us as we really are. In His presence we must throw off our masks and let Him show us who we really are in His sight. Then He can direct us into His will for our life.

*   *   *

"Rejoice with them that do rejoice, and weep with them that weep" (Rom. 12:15).

Sometimes it is easier to weep with them that weep than to rejoice with them that rejoice. It is a temptation to become envious of the blessings that God bestows upon other people. It is but a short step from envy to jealousy, and jealousy can cause division that brings dishonor to the cause of Christ. God has not chosen to deal with us as a body, a group or an assembly, but as individuals; and His dealings with us are fitted to our individual needs. Thank Him for it. Let us rejoice when God's blessings touch a fellow believer, and let us be glad together.

"Dearly beloved, avenge not yourselves, but rather give place unto wrath: for it is written, Vengeance is mine; I will repay, saith the Lord" (Rom. 12:19).

Do you harbor ill feelings against someone and wish to get even? If you do, and carry that grudge, you will never be happy. This is not only harmful to you but is expressly disobedient to the Word of God. It is your responsibility to eliminate these feelings even if you are reluctant to do so. Call your reluctance what it is—*sin*—and pray, "Lord, make me willing to be made willing."

❧   ❧   ❧

"Let every soul be subject unto the higher powers. For there is no power but of God: the powers that be are ordained of God" (Rom. 13:1).

Christ Himself teaches us to "render unto Caesar the things that are Caesar's," as well as "to God the things that are God's." We are to obey and abide by the laws of the land. Civil disobedience is not Christlike, as some would have us believe. Believing in civil rights is not the same as believing in civil wrongs. Christ wants us to be constructive, involved members of our community and our nation, upholding authority, which the Bible tells us is "of God."

"God is faithful, by whom ye were called unto the fellowship of his Son Jesus Christ our Lord" (I Cor. 1:9).

Most Christians believe fellowship is connected with "feeling," but "feeling" is not the basis of fellowship. The English word "fellowship" is a translation of the Greek word *koenonia,* which means "common, community" or "having all things in common." It is the cross that transfers us from holding all things in common with Adam to having all things in common with Christ. He has given you all that He is, so you must give Him all that you are. That's fellowship!

❧　❧　❧

"But the natural man receiveth not the things of the Spirit of God: for they are foolishness unto him: neither can he know them, because they are spiritually discerned" (I Cor. 2:14).

We have all had the experience of trying to share the things of God with someone, only to be met with a complete lack of response. What is so plain to us is seemingly incomprehensible, even ridiculous, to others. We must remember that if God by His Spirit had not revealed His grace and mercy to us, we too would have been as blind and lost as these. Spiritual truth is not learned; it is revealed. We cannot be educated into salvation, but it is revealed to all who will seek.

"For other foundation can no man lay than that is laid, which is Jesus Christ" (I Cor. 3:11).

Children sing a little chorus, with accompanying gestures: "The wise man builds his house upon the rock ....The rains come down and the floods come up .... And the house on the rock stands firm." How true this is. When we build our life upon the great foundation stone, the floods and storms of time may come and go; but we are settled for eternity.

❧   ❧   ❧

"Flee fornication. Every sin that a man doeth is without the body; but he that committeth fornication sinneth against his own body" (I Cor. 6:18).

God must be the Master of our drives or our drives will be the master of us. The worst bondage to be in is the bondage to one's self. What we prize so highly as liberty can end in slavery. Our drives need to be expressed, but they must be subjected to the laws of God. God calls the sin of fornication a sin against the body, and the body is a temple of the Holy Spirit.

"So, dear brothers, in whatever situation a person is when he becomes a Christian, let him stay there, for now the Lord is there to help him" (I Cor. 7:24, Living Letters).

In other words, be a Christian right where you are! Sometimes God has to close every door before we are willing to accept the fact that it is His will for us to remain in just the place we find ourselves. The "grass may look greener on the other side of the fence," but God wants you to be the best possible person in just that situation in which He has put you. Accept this, and you will be fulfilling His highest calling.

❧ ❧ ❧

"Now all these things happened unto them for ensamples: and they are written for our admonition, upon whom the ends of the world are come" (I Cor. 10:11).

There is a strange notion abroad that we do not need to read the Old Testament, as only the New Testament applies to us. It is true that the New Testament is specifically "to" us, but Paul tells us that the Old Testament is certainly "for" us. This is not a collection of interesting folklore, but a depository of great spiritual lessons God has left for us. Peter says that "holy men of God spake as they were moved by the Holy Ghost" (II Peter 1:21). Get to know your Old Testament and see what God has to say to you.

"Wherefore let him that thinketh he standeth take heed lest he fall" (I Cor. 10:12).

Never put confidence in the flesh—yours, or anyone else's. Do not think you are so strong spiritually that it does not matter where you go or whom you're with. It is a law of nature that we eventually take on the color of our environment. It is true that Jesus can keep us from contamination in any situation to which He sends us. But if you think *you* are doing the standing, take heed!

❧ ❧ ❧

"Wherefore let him that thinketh he standeth take heed lest he fall" (I Cor. 10:12).

Never think you have arrived spiritually, for it is in this condition that you are Satan's prime target. He is delighted when you put your confidence in yourself instead of in God. Spiritual smugness is the most dangerous state for a Christian, for it is at this point that he takes his biggest step away from God.

"There hath no temptation taken you but such as is common to man: but God is faithful, who will not suffer you to be tempted above that ye are able; but will with the temptation also make a way to escape, that ye may be able to bear it" (I Cor. 10:13).

Prepositions are often very important in Scripture. Notice the verse reads "with" the temptation, not "out of." We are prone to look for a way out of a difficulty or testing when God's way of escape is often a supply of grace to bear it. Sometimes the only way out is through!

❧ ❧ ❧

"There are diversities of operations, but the same God which worketh all in all" (I Cor. 12:6).

God's high calling differs with each individual. Just as there were different roles in the early church, so it is today. God may call one person into the ministry, another into business, but in His sight each man is in full-time service. God does not call any part-time Christians. Being a Christian is a seven-day-a-week job. Anything we undertake is important and meaningful if God is at the center of it.

"For by one Spirit are we all baptized into one body, whether we be Jews or Gentiles, whether we be bond or free; and have been all made to drink into one Spirit" (I Cor. 12:13).

There is perhaps more confusion among Christians about the doctrine of the Holy Spirit than any other. Some will say, "You need the baptism of the Spirit." If you are a Christian, you have had the baptism of the Holy Spirit at your conversion, and by it you were put into the body of Christ. It is not your position to pray or "tarry" for the Spirit, but thank God you are indwelt by Him. When you received Christ, you received His Spirit. We do not wait for the Spirit, really; He waits for us. Nor do we pray for more of the Spirit (God does not give His Spirit by measure); we need to give Him more of ourselves.

❧   ❧   ❧

"Now ye are the body of Christ, and members in particular" (I Cor. 12:27).

The body of Christ is not an organization but an organism made up of living parts. It is possible to get so wrapped up in the mechanism of "churchianity" that we forget that Christianity is Christ. If Christ is obscured rather than revealed by the structure of "the religious group" in which we find ourselves, we must ask the question, Am I where God wants me to be?

85

"Now ye are the body of Christ, and members in particular" (I Cor. 12:27).

We all, as Christians, are part of the body of Christ. In this passage (chap. 12), Paul shows us how unthinkable it is that one member of our physical body should exalt itself or deem itself unworthy because it differs from another. Though some persons may seem much more gifted in the sight of men, we are all equally valuable and loved in the sight of God. Along with the other gifts of the Spirit mentioned in verse 28, is the gift of "helps." Perhaps this is your gift; if so, do not despise it. It is just as important as the gift of healing, of government, or of diversities of tongues.

❧   ❧   ❧

"Love envieth not . . ." (I Cor. 13:4, ASV).

Most of us would not include envy in a list of gross sins, but let's get God's viewpoint on this. He looks at it far more seriously than we do. He has told us in His Word, "Now the works of the flesh are manifest, which are these; adultery, fornication, uncleanness, lasciviousness, idolatry, witchcraft, hatred, variance, emulations, wrath, strife, seditions, heresies, *envyings,* murders, drunkenness, revellings, and such like: of the which I tell you before, as I have also told you in time past, that they which do such things shall not inherit the kingdom of God" (Gal. 5:19-21). We must not be tolerant where God is not tolerant. Let us put envy out of our lives and permanently forsake it.

"Moreover, brethren, I declare unto you the gospel which I preached unto you, which also ye have received, and wherein ye stand; by which also ye are saved" (I Cor. 15:1-2a).

In these days when words are tossed about so loosely, it is important to be sure we use scriptural definitions of biblical words and concepts. This passage gives an explicit definition of "the gospel." It is that Christ died for our sins, that He was buried and rose again, according to the Scriptures. It is upon receiving this fact that we are saved; it is in believing this fact that we are able to stand as Christians.

❧　❧　❧

"Therefore, my beloved brethren, be ye stedfast, unmoveable, always abounding in the work of the Lord, forasmuch as ye know that your labour is not in vain in the Lord" (I Cor. 15:58).

Today people want to be "where the action is." The slightest incident can distract them from the course God has set for them. Moses threw himself into "the action" by killing an Egyptian, and for that mistake he had to wait forty years on the backside of the desert, learning not to be impetuous and run ahead of God. We must be careful not to be caught up in the emotion of the moment and to be spiritually derailed. God wants us to be in the center of His will, and in that place we will always be "where the action is."

"Who delivered us from so great a death, and doth deliver: in whom we trust that he will yet deliver us" (II Cor. 1:10).

Salvation is a crisis followed by a process. The Bible tells us the "wages of sin is death"; but because Christ took these wages upon Himself and died in our place, we have been delivered (past tense) from the *penalty* of sin. Because Christ arose and triumphed over death, we too can live in "newness of life" and can experience daily deliverance (present tense) from the *power* of sin. Because Christ ascended and is now seated on the right hand of the Father on high, we can look forward to the day when we will be with Him, at last eternally freed from the *presence* of sin.

᪥   ᪥   ᪥

"For all the promises of God in him are yea, and in him Amen, unto the glory of God by us" (II Cor. 1:20).

We often make promises to God under the pressure of circumstances, and quickly forget them when the pressure is removed. Promises made in the flesh are impossible to keep. Don't make promises to God; God alone can keep the promises He makes. We have to stand on *His* promises—not our own—for in Christ all the promises are fulfilled for us.

"Where the Spirit of the Lord is, there is liberty" (II Cor. 3:17*b*).

This is a liberating verse, but we must remember that liberty without discipline degenerates into license. Then we find ourselves in bondage again—to ourselves. In school, the discipline of study sets our minds free. So the disciplines of prayer, meditation and reading of the Word set our spirits free. The happy Christian is one who accepts these disciplines as a way to spiritual liberty ordained by God.

❧ ❧ ❧

"But we all, with open face beholding as in a glass the glory of the Lord, are changed into the same image from glory to glory, even as by the Spirit of the Lord" (II Cor. 3:18).

We all want to be changed—to be more like Jesus, and so we set up all kinds of programs and plans for ourselves whereby this may be accomplished by self-effort. These will be good things in themselves—more prayer time, more Bible study, better personal habits—but they lead to defeat and discouragement. Why? Because change is only brought about by the Holy Spirit as we behold Christ.

"But we have this treasure in earthen vessels, that the excellency of the power may be of God, and not of us" (II Cor. 4:7).

All of us are dispensable and replaceable in God's work. We often think that His purposes cannot be realized without us. Let's not get preoccupied with the vessel. Remember, it is the treasure that the world needs now. Norman Grubb says that an earthen vessel is just a "cracked pot anyway." Our job is to glorify God, not ourselves.

❧   ❧   ❧

"Always bearing about in the body the dying of the Lord Jesus, that the life also of Jesus might be made manifest in our body" (II Cor. 4:10).

Just as Christ was God manifest in the flesh, every Christian is to be Christ manifest in the flesh. What an awesome thought this is! How completely impossible in our own strength! It is only as we see ourselves as "crucified with Christ" (an act), and then "die daily" (a process), that this is accomplished in our lives. May we believe God's Word, that the impossible may become possible in our experience.

"For we walk by faith, not by sight" (II Cor. 5:7).

There is no opposition in the Scriptures between faith and reason, or faith and understanding, but only between faith and sight. God says, "Come let us reason together." God says it is "by faith we understand." But Jesus says, "A wicked and perverse generation seeketh a sign." For what we "see" does not require faith. God has ordained that our walk with Him is not to be by sight but by faith, that our dependence may be upon Him.

❧ ❧ ❧

"Now then we are ambassadors for Christ" (II Cor. 5:20).

An ambassador is one who is personally acquainted with the king and speaks as if the king were speaking. He possesses authority by appointment. We are heavenly ambassadors of our heavenly King, and by His appointment we have authority to speak "in Christ's stead" to a world in need. How well are you representing the King?

"Behold, now is the accepted time; behold, now is the day of salvation" (II Cor. 6:2b).

The moment we are born, we begin to grow and also to die. We have only a short time to live, in contrast to eternity. In a world that moves quickly, we get so caught up with the life here that we forget about the life hereafter. Spiritual decisions are put off with the idea that we will face them later. This self-deception can commit us to a Christless eternity. We must face the reality of God's Son and His provision for our salvation now, for *now* is the accepted time.

❧ ❧ ❧

"Wherefore come out from among them, and be ye separate, saith the Lord, and touch not the unclean thing; and I will receive you" (II Cor. 6:17).

Separation from uncleanliness is always the condition of blessing in the Christian life. We are to be "in" the world but not "of" the world. When we are truly separated "to" God, the separation "from" those things which are contrary to His will and mind take care of themselves. Remember, God does not ask anything of us that He will not enable us to do.

"For the weapons of our warfare are not carnal, but mighty through God to the pulling down of strong holds" (II Cor. 10:4).

First we must realize that the Christian life is not a picnic but a war. If we are to be victorious, we must know what kind of a war we are engaged in and who our enemy is. Ephesians 6:12 tells us that we wrestle not with flesh and blood but against spiritual wickedness. Our trouble is that we spend too much time wrestling with flesh and blood—our own as well as others! We can never win that way, for ours is a spiritual battle, not a fleshly one. If we will just make use of the spiritual weapons that are available to us (prayer and the Word of God), God promises us that Satan's strongholds will fall.

❧   ❧   ❧

"But I fear, lest by any means, as the serpent beguiled Eve through his subtilty, so your minds should be corrupted from the simplicity that is in Christ" (II Cor. 11:3).

There seems to be a great emphasis today upon the philosophical, intellectual and mystical aspects of Christianity, and with it come the traps of pride and affectation. True spirituality is perfectly natural and unassumingly simple. Paul is calling the Galatians to a return to simplicity—a call we could well heed today. He also identifies the corrupter; it is Satan himself.

"As we said before, so say I now again, If any man preach any other gospel unto you than that ye have received, let him be accursed" (Gal. 1:9).

These are strong words, but this was a subject that demanded them. Today we have many voices telling of "another gospel" that the church should be preaching, and many are confused thereby. Let us remember Paul's admonition to preach the gospel of the grace of Christ, and not be led off into other priorities.

⚜ ⚜ ⚜

"Christ liveth in me" (Gal. 2:20).

We do not have a dead Christ hanging on the cross, but a risen Saviour, alive and seated at the right hand of the Father. Just as we are identified with His death, so are we identified with His resurrection. Now it is no longer our life but Christ's life indwelling us. His life is as naturally "good" as our life was naturally "bad." As this life is lived in and through Him, it is as easy to be good "in Christ" as it was to be bad "in Adam." The secret is to believe it.

"Stand fast therefore in the liberty wherewith Christ hath made us free, and be not entangled again with the yoke of bondage" (Gal. 5:1).

We certainly know it was by grace we were saved, and that not of ourselves. Yet, somehow, as we walk the Christian way, we begin to feel that now we must merit and earn our salvation. We think we need to be lovable to be loved, and acceptable to be accepted. Since we are often neither of these things, we become discouraged and even dispairing. We do not realize that we have put ourselves under the law again, which is bondage; and forgotten God's grace, which is liberty. We never could and never can merit God's grace, fortunately.

      ❧   ❧   ❧

"But the fruit of the Spirit is love, joy, peace, long-suffering, gentleness, goodness, faith, meekness, temperance: against such there is no law" (Gal. 5:22).

When we speak of a fruitful Christian life, many people automatically think of an active Christian life. But the fruit that God is the most interested in is not produced by "doing" something but by "being" something. It is the "fruit of the Spirit" working in and through us, not something we—in our natural enthusiasm and ability—put on from the outside. It is true that when we "are" what we should be, we will naturally "do" what we should do; but we must be careful to have the two things in God's proper order.

"Be not deceived; God is not mocked: for whatsoever a man soweth, that shall he also reap" (Gal. 6:7).

Too often we respond to false challenges, and that is exactly what Satan desires us to do. He desires that we use our energies, talents and time for worthy but unimportant spiritual concerns. Don't become side-tracked by such deceit, for that will take a strong spiritual toll on your life.

❧   ❧   ❧

"To the praise of the glory of his grace, wherein he hath made us accepted in the beloved" (Eph. 1:6).

How important it is to everyone of us to be accepted by our friends, our family, but most of all, by God. Unfortunately, our acceptance by our friends and family often fluctuates in proportion to how "acceptable" they find our behavior. Many Christians feel the same is true in their relationship to God. When all is going well, they "feel" accepted; but when they are stumbling, and things seem dry and hard, they no longer feel God loves and accepts them. But God's love and acceptance are unconditional because it is "in the beloved." Our Father may not be fully satisfied with us, but He is fully satisfied with His beloved Son on our behalf. Thank God He has accepted us in His Son, and upon this fact we can rest our faith.

"And you hath he quickened, who were dead in tres-passes and sins" (Eph. 2:1).

Christianity is not a set of rules or a system of theology, but a question of life. Jesus said, "I am . . . the life" (John 14:6), and without Him there is no life. We need to realize that those outside of Christ are spiritually dead. It is our job to minister to them the life-giving truth of the gospel, but we can only do this if Christ is living and vital to us. Are *you* alive in Him?

❧   ❧   ❧

"For by grace are ye saved through faith; and that not of yourselves: it is the gift of God: not of works, lest any man should boast. For we are his workmanship, created in Christ Jesus unto good works, which God hath before ordained that we should walk in them" (Eph. 2:8-10).

We are saved by grace through faith plus nothing. Anything we might add, subtracts from the sacrifice of Christ. As saved people, however, "works" have a large place in our lives. We do not work to "be" saved, but because we "are" saved. Paul tells us to "work out" our salvation, not "work for" our salvation (Phil. 2:12). We are to work out what God has worked in.

"That he would grant you, according to the riches of his glory, to be strengthened with might by his Spirit in the inner man" (Eph. 3:16).

We try to evade disagreeable realities by ignoring or refusing to acknowledge their presence. We may withdraw from certain situations to avoid disagreement, or become too busy with other things to deal with the unpleasant task at hand. We may procrastinate, get "sick," or be "not in the mood" to face the job ahead. Satan would have us in a constant state of fleeing and escaping God's plans for our lives. The longer we try to escape, the more difficult it becomes to face the real issues. Face up to the facts right now in God's strength. He will lead you through the problems.

✻ ✻ ✻

"And grieve not the holy Spirit of God, whereby ye are sealed unto the day of redemption" (Eph. 4:30).

God's Spirit is not called the Holy Spirit for nothing. God's plan for you is that you should live a holy life, and He has given you the Holy Spirit for that purpose. Anything unclean and defiling or degrading grieves Him. What about your thought life? The books you read? The pictures you look at? The stories you listen to? God says, "Grieve not the *Holy* Spirit."

"Redeeming the time, because the days are evil" (Eph. 5:16).

Someone has said, "Procrastination is putting off until tomorrow what you put off until today." Those who meet the Lord sporadically are not ready for Satan's onslaughts. Time is a gift from God—it belongs to Him. It is not our time but *His*. Make time to meet the Lord every day.

     ✿   ✿   ✿

"Children, obey your parents in the Lord: for this is right. Honour thy father and mother; which is the first commandment with promise" (Eph. 6:1-2).

God has commanded us to obey our parents, and Christ gave a reason: for it is right. Honor is more than just obeying; it is a matter of the spirit. Disobedience to parents is not taken lightly by God, but is included in the list of gross sins which will characterize the last days (II Tim. 3:1-4). If we do not honor our parents, we dishonor God, for this is His express desire and command.

"Not with eyeservice, as men-pleasers; but as the servants of Christ, doing the will of God from the heart" (Eph. 6:6).

What is your real motive in doing that Christian service. If you would examine your true inner motivation, what would you find? Are you doing the job for the love of Christ, or for human approbation and self-aggrandizement? We are all so susceptible to the praise of men. Let us not be "men pleasers," but true servants of God, doing His will from a grateful heart.

❧ ❧ ❧

"For we wrestle not against flesh and blood, but against principalities, against powers, against the rulers of the darkness of this world, against spiritual wickedness in high places. Wherefore take unto you the whole armour of God, that ye may be able to withstand in the evil day, and having done all, to stand" (Eph. 6:12-13).

Problems often come into our lives without warning. How we have prepared ourselves before they come, will determine our victory or defeat. Most of our difficulties involve our relationships with other people. Remember, don't wrestle with flesh and blood; put on the whole armor of God *before* the problem arises. This is the secret of the overcoming life.

"And the sword of the Spirit, which is the word of God" (Eph. 6:17*b*).

Some of us are accidents looking for a place to happen. We are prime targets for Satan's attacks and don't realize it. Because we are not in the Book each day, we are not equipped with the sword of the Spirit, the only offensive God offers us against our enemy. When the tests come, we cannot go forward as victors; the best we can do is defend our ground. Are you a "defensive" Christian? If so, get into the Word of God.

❦ ❦ ❦

"Being confident of this very thing, that he which hath begun a good work in you will perform it until the day of Jesus Christ" (Phil. 1:6).

What a wonderful promise this is—that we can be confident of this! This releases us from all the wrestling and striving to produce something in ourselves. It is His work, and He will perform it. This releases us in regard to others also. The good work to be completed in them is God's job; we can't do it, but He can and will. May we rest in this great fact.

"Let this mind be in you, which was also in Christ Jesus" (Phil. 2:5).

This is an instruction to every one of us as Christians: Let this mind be in *you*. And what did this entail? Many things, all of which are foreign and offensive to our natural disposition. What are these things?

1. ". . . made himself of no reputation" (Phil. 2:7). We are so fearful of our reputations, so afraid to appear foolish before the world.
2. "and took upon him the form of a servant" (v. 7). How many of us want to be a servant today?
3. "humbled himself" (v. 8). Humility is considered rather an old-fashioned virtue with many Christians.
4. "obedient unto death" (v. 8). If we are to have the Christ-life, this is what it will take in our experience: obedience unto death of the "self" life.

❧   ❧   ❧

"Do all things without murmurings and disputings" (Phil. 2:14).

If God has called you to a task or put you in a situation which you find distasteful, don't gripe about it. Try to learn what He has for you in it. You can be sure He has called you to be at this place at this time in your life for a reason. To complain is to question the wisdom and goodness of God. He knows better than you do how to run your life. Let Him do it.

"That I may know him, and the power of his resurrection, and the fellowship of his sufferings" (Phil. 3:10a).

Most of us would like to put a period in the middle of this sentence. We want the power, period. Paul knew better. He knew that when we are sufficiently identified with Christ to have experienced His power in our lives, we will also have entered into the fellowship of His suffering. James and John wanted a position of power when they asked to sit on His right and left hand in the kingdom. And Jesus answered them, "Ye know not what ye ask. Are ye able to drink of the cup that I shall drink of . . .?" (Matt. 20:22). Before you pray for power, be sure you know what you ask.

❧ ❧ ❧

"Brethren, I count not myself to have apprehended: but this one thing I do, forgetting those things which are behind, and reaching forth unto those things which are before, I press toward the mark for the prize of the high calling of God in Christ Jesus" (Phil. 3:13-14).

The Christian who is just willing to be average, or just to "get by," is not realizing God's potential for his life. Excellence should be the goal of every Christian; for unless it is, we are selling God short, as well as ourselves. We are not our own, but bought with a price of infinite worth which we dare not underestimate. Remember, identity with the Almighty never produces mediocrity. Let us "press toward the mark . . . of the high calling . . . in Christ Jesus."

"Forgetting those things which are behind, and reaching forth unto those things which are before, I press toward the mark for the prize of the high calling of God in Christ Jesus" (Phil. 3:13b-14).

The past is over; the past is history. The past is written in eternity. The present is ours to fulfill; the future is ours to claim. Satan can try to use our past to undercut our present and future, but God has promised to remember our sins no more. If Satan is striving to throw up confessed and forgiven sins to discourage, put him behind you as the Lord Jesus did when He said to Peter, "Get thee behind me Satan." And "forget those things which are behind."

※　※　※

"Be careful for nothing" (Phil. 4:6).

A friend has a little sign on his desk: "Why pray when you can worry?" Worry is not only useless, it is detrimental and downright sinful. Worry is a sin because every care is a vote of "no confidence" for God. If you trust, you don't worry; and if you worry, you don't trust.

"Be careful for nothing; but in every thing by prayer and supplication with thanksgiving let your requests be made known unto God. And the peace of God, which passeth all understanding, shall keep your hearts and minds through Christ Jesus" (Phil. 4:6-7).

Are you anxious about anything? When anxiety comes in the door, peace goes out the window. God has reminded us to "worry about nothing, pray about everything, and be thankful for anything." Then, and only then, will the peace of God keep your heart and mind through Christ Jesus.

❧ ❧ ❧

"Giving thanks unto the Father, which hath made us meet to be partakers of the inheritance of the saints in light: who hath delivered us from the power of darkness, and hath translated us into the kingdom of his dear Son" (Col. 1:12-13).

Have you ever thanked God for these two tremendous facts: you have been made worthy to be a partaker of the inheritance of the saints in light, and you have been delivered from the power of darkness and have been translated into the kingdom of His dear Son. Never pray to be made worthy or to be delivered. Those two things have already been done for you. Proclaim it to be true, and give thanks!

"And he is the head of the body, the church: who is the beginning, the firstborn from the dead; that in all things he might have the preeminence" (Col. 1:18).

God has given us a proper order and structure for the priority scale of our values, the first of which is our devotion to Christ our Saviour. We can never escape the many demands for our attention, but we can be alert to keep them in proper balance. When we begin to spend more of our time and resources on the other concerns, and neglect our Lord, then we are in trouble in our Christian life. Run a value check on your life and see what things you are giving first attention. If Christ is not number one on the list, that must be remedied right now.

❧ ❧ ❧

"Lie not one to another, seeing that ye have put off the old man with his deeds" (Col. 3:9).

Lying can become almost a way of life, a smoothing over of the rough spots in our relationships with others. We excuse this, calling it a "white lie," but it is inconsistent with the Christian life. Paul tells us why. These are deeds of the "old man," the old way of life. A Christian does not lie, because he is a "new creation in Christ" and the life of Christ is to be manifested in him.

"And whatsoever ye do, do it heartily, as to the Lord, and not unto men" (Col. 3:23).

When we are looking for and expecting the praise of men for the service we render, we are doomed to frustration and disappointment. The thanks we are waiting for seldom, if ever, comes. But when we work to please the Lord, even the most menial of our daily chores can take on new meaning. It is real bondage to be a "man pleaser," but wonderful liberty to be responsible to no one but God. Who are you working for?

❧　❧　❧

"And whatsoever ye do, do it heartily, as to the Lord, and not unto men" (Col. 3:23).

If we cannot obey this command of God through Paul, we need to either change what we are doing, or change our attitude to it. A young woman who hates washing dishes has put these words over her sink: "Not 'somehow,' but triumphantly." This applies to the small "whatsoevers" as well as the big tasks God calls us to do.

"In every thing give thanks: for this is the will of God in Christ Jesus concerning you" (I Thess. 5:18).

Some people find a "bug on every rose," and so they are always dissatisfied. The basis of a Christian spirit is a thankful heart. Without it we cannot be in God's will about anything. This is God's will concerning *you* —not someone else. Accept, believe it, and begin to appreciate what God is doing in your life.

※　※　※

"For God hath not given us the spirit of fear; but of power, and of love, and of a sound mind" (II Tim. 1:7).

Fear engenders weakness, hatred and confusion—the very opposite of the spirit that God gives. If God has not given us the spirit of fear, where does it come from? Directly from Satan, the enemy of our souls. When we know this, we can reject fear as being from the enemy, and confidently state that God *has* given us the spirit of power, and love and a sound mind, and they are ours to appropriate in any given situation.

"For God hath not given us the spirit of fear; but of power, and of love, and of a sound mind" (II Tim. 1:7).

These are days when truly "men's hearts [are] failing them for fear," as prophesied in Luke 21:26. As we look at the world around us, there is more than ample provocation. But to those of us who are "in Christ," there is no cause for fear, regardless of circumstances. Indeed, we are told categorically that God has *not* given us the spirit of fear. If He has not given that spirit to us, it must come from either the world or the flesh or the devil. When we recognize this, we can reject fear by the Spirit He *has* given us. This is the Holy Spirit, which is the spirit of power, love and a sound mind.

❧ ❧ ❧

"There remaineth therefore a rest to the people of God" (Heb. 4:9).

How is your pressure level today? When it begins, pressure can mount at an alarming rate. We reach a point where we can no longer see life in its true proportion. We can never escape pressure, but we can relieve pressure. This is accomplished by a moment-by-moment surrender of ourselves to God. Then life becomes a "resting" rather than a "wrestling."

"He ever liveth to make intercession for them" (Heb. 7:25*b*).

The book of Hebrews tells us we have a great High Priest in heaven, and His present ministry is one of intercession. He is praying for us and will be praying with us if we enter into this ministry with Him. What an encouragement it is to pray when we realize we do not pray alone but join a prayer meeting already going on in heaven!

❧ ❧ ❧

"Now faith is the assurance (the confirmation, the title-deed) of the things [we] hope for, being the proof of things [we] do not see and the conviction of their reality—faith perceiving as real fact what is not revealed to the senses" (Heb. 11:1, Amplified).

Biblical faith and the "power of positive thinking" are definitely not the same thing, though many confuse the two. Faith is not thinking that if we believe something hard enough we can bring it to pass. Faith must be based on fact—the fact and certainty of God's Word. Faith without such a basis is nothing more than superstition or presumption. *Our* faith is nothing; it is what we have our faith *in* that counts. Step out on faith in the facts of God's Word.

"But without faith it is impossible to please him: for he that cometh to God must believe that he is, and that he is a rewarder of them that diligently seek him" (Heb. 11:6).

God says that nothing we do pleases Him unless we have faith. Somehow we understand this for the initial act of believing God for salvation, but we fail to see it for the Christian walk. Actually, God gives everything in answer to our faith. God has given us all things in Christ. All we have to do is believe it to make it real in our lives.

❧   ❧   ❧

"And these all, having obtained a good report through faith . . ." (Heb. 11:39a).

Today we hear a great deal about "situational ethics" which means, in a word, that the situation entirely determines how you behave. Some would tell you that the biblical absolutes are only relative in this age. The whole of Hebrews 11 is God's object lesson to us that the life of faith is possible in any age under *any circumstances*. "These all" were believers who trusted God in a diversity of impossible situations and thereby obtained a "good report" from Him. God always knows your situation and gives grace equal to it if you believe Him for it.

"Let us lay aside every weight and the sin which does so easily beset us" (Heb. 12:1).

It is very easy to fall into the same pattern of behavior that started us previously on our spiritual descent. These patterns can creep into our lives very quietly and subtly. They can appear at very inopportune times and then at quite obvious times. Mark Twain wrote of the frog that was in the pan being boiled, and the process was so slow that it didn't realize its condition until it was burned. So it can be with our "besetting sins." Therefore, we must be careful not to subject ourselves to conditions that eventually will ensnare us. Even though we have confessed our deviance from God, it does not mean that we will never deviate again.

"Let us lay aside every weight, and the sin which doth so easily beset us, and let us run with patience the race that is set before us" (Heb. 12:1*b*).

Paul's picture is of a runner intent upon his performance in a race. If we are serious about our performance in the Christian "race," we, too, must lay aside the things which hold us back. These "weights" may not necessarily be sinful in themselves; but if God the Holy Spirit puts His finger on them as impeding our spiritual progress, they must go. A good rule to remember in this regard is, If it doesn't help, it *does* hinder. Ask yourself, Does it send me on, or does it hold me back? Act accordingly.

❧ ❧ ❧

"Looking unto Jesus the author and finisher of our faith" (Heb. 12:2*a*).

Christianity is not to be judged by the church or its people, but should be judged by the person of Christ. Christians are all in a growing process and at best can project only a partial image of Christ. Don't let inconsistencies in the lives of others hinder your own growth. Remember, while you are looking at their lives, they are also looking at yours. Your concern is to look unto Jesus, not unto men. They will always fail you. He never will.

113

"Ye have not yet resisted unto blood, striving against sin" (Heb. 12:4).

When we get a little persecution or pressure, it is easy to fall into a state of martyrdom and self-pity. At this point we need to put our lives under the searchlight of God's Word and ask ourselves, How difficult are my problems, really? How many are of my own making? Could they be eliminated if I brought my life into line with God's will? We need only to compare our circumstances with the circumstances of early Christians, to whom these words were written, to realize how little "striving against sin" we do.

❧   ❧   ❧

"Now no chastening for the present seemeth to be joyous, but grievous: nevertheless afterward it yieldeth the peaceable fruit of righteousness unto them which are exercised thereby" (Heb. 12:11).

Think of the athlete who exercises and trains in order to harden flabby muscles and to condition himself to meet his opponent. There may be much fatigue and many aches and pains which he willingly endures to accomplish his goal. Spiritually, think of God as a coach who knows our weaknesses and is putting us through just that kind of spiritual exercise that we need to meet *our* opponent and accomplish *our* goal. There may be fatigue and pain, but these we will willingly endure if His goal is our goal—"the peaceable fruit of righteousness."

"When all kinds of trials and temptations come into your lives, my brothers, don't resent them as intruders, but welcome them as friends! Realize that they have come to test your faith and to produce in you the quality of endurance" (James 1:2-3, Phillips).

God has not isolated the Christian from life. Life's conflicts and responsibilities automatically produce times of hardship and trouble. But times of trouble are times of growth. Satan wants us to consider these periods as punishment from God, but God intends them for our help. Welcome these periods of trial, and learn their important lessons. If we constantly ask why, God will be unable to achieve His goals in us.

"Let no man say when he is tempted, I am tempted of God: for God cannot be tempted with evil, neither tempteth he any man: but every man is tempted, when he is drawn away of his own lust, and enticed. Then when lust hath conceived, it bringeth forth sin: and sin, when it is finished, bringeth forth death" (James 1:13-15).

Never say you are tempted of God; you are always tempted through your own lust. Lust is the inordinate affectation we give to anything—good or bad. Even a "good" thing can become a temptation if it is not put in the proper perspective. This then becomes sin. God has equipped us to meet temptation through His Word and the Holy Spirit. We need to be led, not by the tempter, Satan, but by the Victor, Christ.

❧ ❧ ❧

"Be ye doers of the word, and not hearers only, deceiving your own selves" (James 1:22).

Just as it is possible to have a lack of knowledge of Christ and not be a possessor of His life, so it is possible to know "all about" the Christian life and still not live it. In this we deceive ourselves but no one else; it is always very obvious to those about us. Have you become "gospel hardened" by too much "hearing" it and not enough "doing" it? Confess your hardness of heart to God; He has promised to give you a new heart.

116

"Even so the tongue is a little member, and boasteth great things. Behold, how great a matter a little fire kindleth! But the tongue can no man tame; it is an unruly evil, full of deadly poison" (James 3:5, 8).

Our tongue can be a source of great virtue or a vehicle of great harm. We too often speak before we think and then find ourselves apologizing because of our blunders. Though forgiveness is obtained from the individual we harmed, our words may never be forgotten. Long-standing friendships can be severed with just a few words. Learn to speak not only as you would want someone to speak to you, but as you believe God has guided you. "A word fitly spoken is like apples of gold in pictures of silver" (Prov. 25:11).

"That the trial of your faith, being much more precious than of gold that perisheth, though it be tried with fire, might be found unto praise and honour and glory at the appearing of Jesus Christ" (I Peter 1:7).

God never told us that the Christian life was going to be all "hearts and flowers," but somehow we have gotten that idea. When the road gets rough and lonely and discouraging we begin to wonder, Is it worth it after all? God says this very trial of our faith is indeed worth a great deal in His sight; it is more precious than gold that perisheth. His viewpoint is so different from ours; He sees the end from the beginning. When the spiritual going gets hard, remember that God says these very hard things are going to be found to be praise and honor and glory. "It *will* be worth it all, when we see Jesus."

"For what glory is it, if, when ye be buffeted for your faults, ye shall take it patiently? But if, when ye do well, and suffer for it, ye take it patiently, this is acceptable with God" (I Peter 2:20).

Our feelings are hurt so easily. Satan is delighted when we take this position because then we are acting entirely in the flesh. "Hurt feelings" are sin because they are *self*-centered, not Christ-centered. In this, as in all things, we should follow our Lord's example. Regardless of the provocation, He refused to take offense. So it can be with us, and in so doing we may enter into the "fellowship of His suffering."

❧   ❧   ❧

"For what glory is it, if, when ye be buffeted for your faults, ye shall take it patiently? But if, when ye do well, and suffer for it, ye take it patiently, this is acceptable with God" (I Peter 2:20).

It is easy for us to understand that when we are wrong we will be criticized, but how hard it is to be "buffeted" when we are right. It may be a stand on an issue, a question of morality or ethics, or a situation in which our good intentions have been completely misunderstood. As a Christian, what do you do? The answer is, "What did Jesus do?" When "he was reviled, reviled not again" (v. 23). He never defended Himself, although He was always right. If you defend yourself, God can't defend you. If you don't, He has to.

119

"Beloved, think it not strange concerning the fiery trial which is to try you, as though some strange thing happened unto you" (I Peter 4:12).

Christianity is not a vaccination that makes you immune from the germs of life. Sin is still rampant, and we will be exposed to its effects until eternity. The Christian experience is not all "joy bells ringing in your heart." We are subject to pressures from the world, the flesh and the devil. But if we are prepared and are utilizing the means of grace God has given us, we will not be defeated. We are to expect these trials and to be victorious in them.

❧ ❧ ❧

"Casting all your care upon him; for he careth for you" (I Peter 5:7).

Repression is a defensive reaction by which we exclude painful thoughts from our consciousness so that we are no longer aware of them. This is a dangerous situation, for these things go unsolved and, more importantly, they go unconfessed. As Christians, we can face these problems rather than repress them. What we cannot handle, God can. Take your troubles to the Lord and leave them there.

"According as his divine power hath given unto us all things that pertain unto life and godliness, through the knowledge of him that hath called us to glory and virtue: whereby are given unto us exceeding great and precious promises: that by these ye might be partakers of the divine nature, having escaped the corruption that is in the world through lust" (II Peter 1:3-4).

One reason for the barrenness of our Christian experience is that we are always asking for things we already have, and trying to produce what God has already given. God "*hath* given [past tense] . . . all things that pertain unto life"—that is, salvation and "godliness"— that is the Christian walk. Stop asking and start taking. Get acquainted with God's exceeding great and precious promises, and appropriate them for your very own. They are written to you!

"Whereby are given unto us exceeding great and precious promises: that by these ye might be partakers of the divine nature, having escaped the corruption that is in the world through lust" (II Peter 1:4).

So often we hear Christians excusing some unChrist-like behavior with these words: "Well, after all, it's only human nature." Through the regenerating power of the Holy Spirit in the new birth, they have been made "partakers of the divine nature" and possess all the attributes thereof. We can choose to display this nature which is ours through the power of the indwelling Christ. There is no excuse for a Christian displaying "only human nature."

❧ ❧ ❧

"But if we walk in the light, as he is in the light, we have fellowship one with another, and the blood of Jesus Christ his Son cleanseth us from all sin" (I John 1:7).

"Walking in the light" means being honest about ourselves with God and with our fellowman. It means not pretending to be something spiritually that we really aren't, not being a Christian "phony." It is only as we are real with other people that we truly have fellowship. It is only as we are real with God that we can be cleansed from sin.

"If we say that we have no sin, we deceive ourselves, and the truth is not in us" (I John 1:8).

Our self-deception and protective mechanisms are so great that it is actually possible to see ourselves without sin. Of course, we realize we have our little faults like everyone else, but we do not see ourselves as sinners worthy of death. This keeps us from the knowledge of real truth in every area of our life, and leads to deadness and lack of reality in our Christian experience. We need to agree with God's estimate of our condition and to get ourselves back in the proper perspective with Him.

❧　❧　❧

"If we say that we have no sin, we deceive ourselves, and the truth is not in us" (I John 1:8).

God can't forgive excuses; God only forgives sins. When we rationalize and defend our sins instead of calling them what they are, we cannot hope to have true communion with the Lord. Jesus said, "I am the truth," and no deception can stand in His presence. Let us clean out the closets of our hearts and minds, confess our sins, and receive the forgiveness God so freely gives.

"If we confess our sins, he is faithful and just to for-give us our sins, and to cleanse us from all unrighteous-ness" (I John 1:9).

If we pile on one unconfessed sin after another, we are in trouble. The psychiatrist's answer to this is to talk through these experiences. The Lord, however, in-vites us to confess our sins to Him. We must learn to pray and confess to the Lord with true openness the minute these things appear. Begin praying in this way now, with openness to the Lord, and your life will change. Keep short accounts with God. Don't let the garbage pile up.

☙ ☙ ☙

"If we say that we have not sinned, we make him a liar, and his word is not in us" (I John 1:10).

"Sin" is not a popular word or concept today. Some would have us do away with it altogether. But God believes in sin; and if we believe His Word, we must believe in it as well. As someone has said, "Our prob-lem has been 'absolutizing' the relatives, which has led to 'relativizing' the absolutes." Because there have been so many false standards, the trend now is to no standards. The Christian can maintain his equilibrium spiritually by being sure his absolutes agree with God's.

"For this purpose the Son of God was manifested, that he might destroy the works of the devil" (I John 3:8*b*).

We must never laugh at or underestimate the enemy of our souls. He was important enough to make it necessary for Christ to come to the earth to undo his work. But neither need we fear him, for Christ *did* come and has destroyed sin (Satan's work) at the cross. The devil is a defeated foe when we claim Calvary's victory in our lives.

❦   ❦   ❦

"These things have I written unto you that believe on the name of the Son of God; that ye may know that ye have eternal life, and that ye may believe on the name of the Son of God" (I John 5:13).

If you should be asked, "Are you a Christian?" never say, "I hope so," or "I'm trying to be." God says you can *know*. If you say you "hope so" you are not believing Him. What are you hoping for? God has done it all in Christ. If you say you are "trying to be," you have not taken God at His word. Making you a Christian is His job, and He has already done it if you have believed in His Son.

"Save some by snatching them as from the very flames of hell itself. And as for others, help them to find the Lord by being kind to them, but fear the possibility of being pulled along into their sins. Hate every trace of their sin while being merciful to them as sinners" (Jude 23, Living Letters).

You don't need to experience sin to know sin. God has given us a complete picture of it in His Word. Don't be drawn through naïveté into involvement with evildoing, trying to "save" evildoers. True, God loves the sinner, but He hates sin. Let's be sure we also hate sin.